Joseph R. Conlin is Associate Professor of History at Chico State College, Chico, California. Since receiving his Ph.D. from the University of Wisconsin in 1966, Professor Conlin has published two other books, *American Antiwar Movements* (1968) and *Big Bill Haywood and the Radical Union Movement* (1969), and has contributed a number of articles to scholarly journals.

David A. Shannon, Dean of Faculty at the University of Virginia, is one of America's foremost historians specializing in labor and economic history. Among Dean Shannon's published works are *Between the Wars: America, 1919-1941; Progressivism and Post War Disillusionment; Socialist Party of America;* and *Twentieth Century America.*

BREAD AND ROSES TOO

CONTRIBUTIONS IN
AMERICAN HISTORY

SERIES EDITOR

STANLEY I. KUTLER
Department of History
University of Wisconsin

BREAD AND ROSES TOO

Studies of the Wobblies

*CONTRIBUTIONS IN
AMERICAN HISTORY*
Number One

Joseph Robert Conlin

Greenwood Publishing Corporation

WESTPORT, CONNECTICUT

Greenwood Publishing Corporation
51 Riverside Avenue, Westport, Connecticut 06880

Greenwood Publishing Ltd.
42 Hanway Street, London, W.1., England

Printed in the United States of America

Designed by Nina Greenstein

TO EAMONN

As we come marching in the beauty of the day
A million darkened kitchens, a thousand mill-lofts
    gray,
Are touched with all the radiance that a sudden
    sun discloses,
For the people hear us singing: "Bread and Roses!
    Bread and Roses!"

—BREAD AND ROSES *by James Oppenheim,
*inspired by a banner carried by a
Wobbly girl on strike in Lawrence,
Massachusetts, in 1912, which read, "We
Want Bread and Roses Too!"*

Foreword

FOR a relatively small labor organization that had all but disappeared before it was twenty years old, the Industrial Workers of the World has attracted unusual attention among scholars, journalists, and writers of fiction. In the half century since the IWW's virtual demise, hardly a year has passed without a book or article that has treated the organization some way or another. The persistence of this interest is remarkable. It seems to go beyond interest in other "lost causes" of comparable size and influence.

Part of the continued interest in the Wobblies, of course, is due to the great number of colorful characters among their leaders. The IWW was good copy; it still is. A man like Bill Haywood is difficult to forget. But it is likely that a more profound source of interest in the IWW lies in the contrast between what the American labor movement has become and what the IWW was.

As the mainstream of the American labor movement has developed, first in the AFL, then in the CIO, and since 1955 in the AFL-CIO, there have been many intellectuals who have dissented from the movement's ideology, tactics, and general style. Some of the dissenters have seen in the IWW qualities they wish existed in the dominant labor movement. As unions have sought to improve their members' wages, hours, and working conditions but accepted with little question the general economic framework within which labor

works, some dissenters have looked back a bit wistfully at
the Wobblies, who wanted more for labor in the capitalistic
short run and the establishment of a socialist economy as
well. Further, at least since the late 1930s, the labor movement
has only infrequently shown a concern for civil liberty approaching the intensity of the Wobblies' interest in such matters. Critics of the labor movement have also regarded it as
not sufficiently militant and imaginative tactically, no match
for the never-say-die firebrands of the IWW.

But perhaps the general style of the main labor movement,
particularly its bureaucracy, has offended its critics more than
anything else, and here the contrast with the IWW is particularly strong. Every AFL-CIO union has a large, specialized,
and generally well-paid staff; the IWW had no staff even
remotely comparable, and Wobblies rejected the idea of sal-
aried union employees as "porkchopping." To them the notion
of paying a union officer a salary that would be respectable
among corporation officials was unthinkable. The men who
founded the IWW in the proletarian plainness of Brand's
Hall in Chicago would be appalled by the corporate atmosphere of the AFL-CIO Building in Washington, a glassy, slick
structure that has Muzak in its carpeted elevators. And the
IWW delegates who went to Chicago in freight cars would be
dubious about the jet flights to today's labor conventions in
Miami Beach.

It has been rather easy for the critics of what the labor
movement has become to romanticize the Wobblies, to see in
them the embodiment of working-class virtues they consider
missing in the contemporary movement. (Liberal and radical
intellectuals are by no means unique in tending to romanticize
aspects of the past. Witness those who chafe under the grubby
complexities of urban life and romanticize the cowboy, that

paragon of noble manliness who rode under a sky that was ever blue and to whom every day was Saturday.) Writers of fiction, less constrained by historical evidence than historians and other scholars, have long romanticized the IWW, its leaders, and its members. Jack London, only a few years after the IWW's founding, wrote a terrible short story entitled "The Dream of Debs," which was as inaccurate about IWW goals as it was about Debs's actual views on social revolution. Upton Sinclair in *Jimmie Higgins* (1919) had a Wobbly character he romanticized to the point of caricature. John Dos Passos emphasized Bill Haywood's romantic qualities in his sketch of him in *The 42nd Parallel*. But some historians, too, have been guilty of romanticizing the IWW, although to a lesser extent and when the Wobblies have not been the central subject of their writing. One recent general history of American labor called Haywood "a Bunyanesque figure" and referred to the Wobblies collectively as "the troubadours of discontent."

However, there is another tradition of academic writing about the IWW that is anything but romantic. Having its roots in German "scientific" historical writing and French positivist thought, American scholarship has too often resulted in a dry-as-dust writing that piles "fact" upon "fact," avoids interpretation, reveals little understanding, and overuses the passive voice. Some of this scholarly product has as little literary flair as a chemistry laboratory report. A great deal of the labor history that has come from the pens of university scholars is in this tradition, and this is a puzzling matter since the subject is full of drama and passion. The pioneering work on the IWW, Paul F. Brissenden's *The IWW: A Study of American Syndicalism,* which remains after fifty years the most important comprehensive treatment and the basic book with which a serious investigator must begin, is in this tradition. Wallace Stegner, himself the author of a very good novel about Joe Hill, *The Preacher and the Slave,* was quite right about many scholarly works on the IWW when he commented that they "lack the kind of poetic understanding which should invest any history of a militant church."

Happily, Joseph R. Conlin has given us in this book a series of essays that have the necessary poetic understanding, that do not romanticize the Wobblies, and that are well written and interesting. Conlin clarifies our thinking about the IWW and corrects some common and basic misinterpretations. These essays are a truly major contribution. No one interested in the IWW can afford to ignore them.

A final comment: Professor Conlin tells us that "the Wobblies were in reality more like than unlike their conventional contemporaries" and that "the IWW moved with the American mainstream at least as regularly as it bucked the current." Let us hope that readers in considering this thesis and other ideas in the book will focus on the merits of the case and not involve themselves in nonsense about consensus *or* conflict, an argument that often as not becomes confused with contemporary political issues and what one thinks should be, rather than what was or is, the actual situation. It seems axiomatic that in almost all human relations there is some consensus *and* some conflict.

DAVID A. SHANNON

Contents

Preface

FIVE years ago, when I began to research and write about the Industrial Workers of the World, the last comprehensive study of the subject was nearly fifty years old. I had, and still have, great respect for the volume, Paul F. Brissenden's *The IWW: A Study of American Syndicalism*. Few historical phenomena have had so competent a chronicler so soon. But I thought that the compilation over half a century of new sources and the device of new historical methods merited new labors in the field.

During the last five years, new works have indeed been published; one might almost speak of a Wobbly revival among historians. One of America's foremost labor historians, Philip S. Foner, has written a detailed narrative history of the IWW. A British journalist, Patrick Renshaw, has contributed a highly readable popular account. Robert S. Tyler has studied IWW activities in a specific region, the Pacific Northwest. And the journals have presented a spate of articles.

All of which might have effectively sealed the gap in the field from which the excellence of Brissenden's scholarship had frightened historians. Indeed, Foner's and Tyler's painstaking works seem to preclude the writing of another narrative history for the time being. But both of them and most of the other recent students of the IWW have failed to correct some basic errors of interpretation handed down from the days when the Wobblies were grist for the headlines. This book attempts to supply the remedy.

This is an analytical study. While an introductory narrative hopefully provides sufficient information to make the analysis intelligible to the reader only superficially acquainted with the Wobbly story, the book is designed as a supplement to, rather than a successor of, the works of Brissenden, Foner, Renshaw, Tyler, and others. It is organized topically; the chapters constitute something of an essay sequence, structured around the central problems with which the IWW confronts historians. I have no illusions that I have had the last word. I changed my mind and reversed my field too many times during the course of researching and writing this study to indulge in any aspirations of finality. I am happy merely that at one point in the process this study satisfied me sufficiently to submit it to others' scrutiny.

I have the usual obligations to note. My thanks go to the librarians and archivists of the State Historical Society of Wisconsin, the Minnesota Historical Society, the National Archives, the Labadie Collection of the University of Michigan, the Labor History Archives of Wayne State University, the Tamiment Institute, the Socialist Party Collection at Duke University, the University of California Library at Berkeley, and the Hoover Institution at Stanford University.

To Wobblies Fred Thompson and Carl Keller of Chicago

and Richard Brazier of New York City I repeat previous thanks for their many courtesies extended and information proffered. Mr. Virgil Vogel of Chicago permitted me to read his valuable manuscript on "The Historians and the IWW." Mr. Michael Ebner of the University of Virginia has corresponded with me on the subject and opened my eyes in a number of matters.

My first serious study of the IWW was presented as a doctoral dissertation at the University of Wisconsin, written under the direction of Professor Richard N. Current. He and professors E. David Cronon and Eric Lampard of the same institution advised me in the expurgation of many gaucheries and errors. To those cronies who also read parts of this book in one form or another, I also repeat my thanks: Thomas Wagstaff, Steven Anderson, and William P. Friedheim. They know already with how much of this study they dissent and need no public absolution of responsibility.

Finally, my gratitude to those editors of journals who permitted me to reproduce here parts of essays originally written for them. Theses advanced in Chapter 1 appeared in abbreviated form in *Studies on the Left* as "Wobblies and Syndicalists." Parts of Chapter 3 appeared previously as "Afterthoughts on the Wobblies" in *The American West*. A section of Chapter 4 is taken from "The IWW and the Question of Violence," which appeared in the *Wisconsin Magazine of History*, and Chapter 5 is substantially unchanged from "The IWW and the Socialist Party" in *Science and Society*.

Mrs. Jean L. Harvey prepared the final typescript, and a Chancellor's Leave from the State Colleges of California provided time to prepare the final manuscript.

JOSEPH ROBERT CONLIN

Introduction

Chicago's Brand's Hall, a favorite meeting place of the anarchists of the Black International during the 1880s, had been the scene of many a tumultuous gathering. The Lake Street edifice was a favorite object of police surveillance. By 1905, however, Brand's was twenty years past its heyday. The Chicago anarchists, once so prominent as to attract the attention of Mikhail Bakunin himself, had been discredited and dispersed in the aftermath of the Haymarket incident of 1886. But, despite its declined fortunes, the building was to shelter one more historic assemblage.

On June 27, 1905, William Dudley "Big Bill" Haywood of the Western Federation of Miners walked to the platform of the hall to face a noisy crowd. There were anarchists, of course, in all their varieties; no meeting at Brand's could escape the notice of the anarchists. And there were socialists of every hue of red: members of the Socialist Labor party, including the party's undisputed leader, Daniel De Leon; representatives of the young but vital Socialist party of America; and many self-styled socialists who were affiliated with neither. Former populists sat in the hall as did hardheaded trade union organizers with no sectarian associations.

This motley crowd was dignified as an "Industrial Union Congress" and presented Chairman Haywood with a problem of protocol. How to address such a diversity? "Brothers and Sisters" was reminiscent of Samuel Gompers' conservative American Federation of Labor. If there was one point upon which the assembled could agree, it was the moral bankruptcy of the AFL. "Comrades" would offend the few nonsocialists present. "Ladies and Gentlemen" was singularly unproletarian. Haywood apparently did not resolve his petty dilemma until, at ten o'clock sharp, he looked briefly for a gavel, found none, and substituted a length of board that was handy. *"Fellow Workers,"* he shouted, "this is the Continental Congress of the Working Class."

Although the new organization was not named for several days, this marked the founding of the Industrial Workers of the World, climaxing a season of moderate fury on the American Left. Late in 1904, six radical union leaders held a series of discussions in Chicago on the state of the labor movement. They invited some thirty others to a conference at Brand's in January. The group included Algie M. Simons, editor of the *International Socialist Review;* William D. Haywood and Charles Moyer of the Western Federation of Miners; Mother Mary Jones of the United Mine Workers; twice presidential candidate, Eugene V. Debs; Father Thomas J. Hagerty, at the peak of his brief career as an organizer; and Frank Bohn, a disciple of Daniel De Leon. After extensive talks, they issued a Manifesto consisting of a Marxian exposition of "the great facts of present industry" and the convention call.

Out of the convention emerged an organization which lived the short but brilliant career of a comet. And out of the Manifesto and the convention harangues emerged a coherent philosophy of labor unionism that stood basically unchanged until the World War.

The IWW's "revolutionary industrial unionism" cannot be understood without reference to the American Federation of Labor. The union was organized in conscious reaction to Samuel Gompers' design for the American working class and offered an alternative to the AFL at practically every point of its program. The IWW was revolutionary, first of all; the union abjured the AFL's acceptance of capitalist economy and called instead for the abolition of the system and the institution of a socialist commonwealth. "The working class and the employing class have nothing in common," the Wobblies stated unequivocally enough in the famous Preamble, "There can be no peace so long as hunger and want are found among millions of working people, and the few, who make up the employing class, have all the good things of life."

But the IWW was also a more conventional union, recognizing that the revolution was not imminent and that, in the meantime, it must get at least some of the "good things" for the workers. Where the AFL was a loose federation of virtually autonomous unions, however, the IWW was to be centralized, in recognition of the centralization of American capital and industry. The IWW was also like the Congress of Industrial Organizations thirty years later, organized along *industrial* lines. "The employers' lines of battle and methods of warfare correspond to the solidarity of the mechanical and industrial concentration, while laborers still form their fighting organizations on lines of long-gone trade divisions," read the Manifesto in reference to the AFL's organization according to craft. To the IWW, such divisions "foster political ignorance among the workers, thus dividing their class at the ballot box, as well as in the shop, mine and factory." All workers in a given industry belonged to the same union in the IWW.

Implicit in the notion of industrial organization was the inclusion of unskilled workers, whom the AFL regarded as unorganizable. Indeed, the organization of the unskilled and other groups traditionally overlooked or excluded in many AFL unions—immigrants, Negroes, women—became an IWW priority. "What we want to establish at this time," William D. Haywood told the convention in his opening address, "is a labor organization that will open wide its doors to every man that earns his livelihood either by his brain or his muscle." Wobblies excoriated the AFL's concept of an aristocracy of labor in every particular. It was to be no mere special-interest group but a class organization, a mass movement.

The founding convention adjourned amidst high spirits but, in fact, the IWW's first three years were dismal at best. Although the union fought a few small strikes immediately, the organization dissipated its energies internally in factional struggles for control. The battles were fought with a bitterness that belied their lack of ideological content and bore little relationship to the meager prize at stake.

The IWW's weakness was that, while its charter members agreed on basic principles and program, they harbored deep personal animosities toward one another. Rivalry between the Socialist party of America and the Socialist Labor party erupted during the summer of 1906 to split the little union into two rival groups, one of which, headed by President Charles O. Sherman, gave up the ghost in 1907. Chagrined by this development, the IWW's largest component, the Western Federation of Miners, left the IWW. In 1908, the movement split once again when nonpolitical unionists, led by Vincent St. John, a Western Federationist who remained with the IWW, forced the Socialist Laborites into bolting.

Then, in 1909, none too soon for the weakened union, Wobblies in Spokane, Washington, made national headlines when they forced the city to back down from its attempt to muzzle the IWW's organizational work among migrant workers. And the IWW led steelworkers in McKees Rocks, Pennsylvania, to a victory over the Pressed Steel Car Works of that city. The IWW fought a number of "free speech fights" between 1909 and 1916, principally in western towns. The fights followed a pattern. Town governors, alarmed by the increasing Wobbly presence and goaded by interests toward whom the IWW was especially hostile (in Spokane it was fraudulent employment agencies), passed ordinances rescinding rights of public speech and assembly in areas where migrant workers gathered. To the IWW, the soapbox was the lifeline of its propaganda, and the Wobblies combated the ordinances by defiance. They spoke, were arrested, and filled the jails. They clogged the judicial process in the hope of making prosecution so expensive that repeal of the obnoxious law was more expedient than enforcement. And they won in a remarkable number of cases.

The eastern strikes also followed something of a pattern in that the IWW actually called very few of them. The rule—in McKees Rocks, in Lawrence, Massachusetts, in 1912, in Akron in 1913, in Paterson the same year, and in a dozen lesser cases —was a spontaneous walkout followed by a popular summons of IWW leadership. The Wobbly-led strikes were fought with revolutionary rhetoric for immediate gains and they were non-violent, relying instead on solidarity (the Wobblies' magic word) and mass picketing. Fought by the very unskilled immigrants whom the AFL spurned, the strikes were often successful, the greatest victory of all at Lawrence in 1912. But Lawrence was followed by a harsh defeat in the silk-weaving town of Paterson in 1913 and, except for an IWW union among Philadelphia longshoremen, the IWW never quite regained the eastern prestige it claimed after Lawrence.

The story was different among the migrant workers of the West, men who manned the forests and sawmills, followed the harvests, and worked the construction sites. Abandoning the tactic of the "free speech fight" in 1915 and 1916, the IWW devised a new means of organization, job delegates. These were union activists who, unpaid, organized on the job as they worked. Wobbly leaders estimated that there were as many as 5,000 job delegates in the field at one time. The Agricultural Workers' Organization became the single most powerful branch of the union.

By early 1917, when the United States entered the World War, the IWW seemed almost established on the American industrial scene. It had outlived and outgrown the most destructive aspects of its factionalism. It seemed to be weathering the shrill cries of its enemies that the union was destructively "anarchistic" and violent. Ill feeling between the IWW and the SPA appeared to have proved not mortal. Membership was increasing slowly and stabilizing. The union already had a "history" of a few glorious victories and colorful martyrs like Joe Hill, who incidentally had provided the IWW with the songs that comprised part of its vital élan.

But the war proved a disaster, not unforeseen by their secretary-treasurer, William D. Haywood. Fearing the repression that eventually drove him into exile and the IWW into obscurity, Haywood attempted to accommodate his revolutionary union to the times. But to no avail. In a series of "sedition" trials (the largest, at Chicago, saw 101 Wobblies sentenced to long prison terms), the IWW's leadership was emasculated and its membership dispersed. While the organization survived the war, it was not the vital revolutionary industrial union of 1912. Controlled by anarcho-syndicalists who, paradoxically, seemed to eschew practical labors while they planned in great detail the techniques by which they would operate industry in the cooperative commonwealth, the IWW drifted into senility by the mid-1920s. The organization still survives today, maintains a few "haunted halls" about the country, and publishes a monthly newspaper, *The Industrial Worker.*

1

A Name That Leads to Confusion

ALTHOUGH the IWW was founded in 1905, few outside America's tiny radical clique knew that such an organization existed until 1909 when the Wobblies became "news" as a result of their antics in the West Coast free speech fights. There had been cursory notices of IWW conventions in the largest daily newspapers, usually as column fillers, and a periodic snarl or snicker from Samuel Gompers' editorials in the *American Federationist* but little more.

Suddenly in 1909, the IWW was the subject of a great deal of excited newspaper copy and soon after the first editions, a deluge of authoritative explanations of just where the new movement had come from. Especially during 1912 and 1913 the popular magazines were filled with explanatory articles, and booksellers were advertising many volumes about the IWW, the "new unionism," and syndicalism.[1]

There was some disagreement about the origins of the

IWW, but within a few years one point of consensus emerged: the IWW was the American branch of a movement then sweeping over parts of Europe, Australia, South Africa, and Latin America, namely, syndicalism. The term had a sinister sound to it and was, indeed, to be taken very seriously. (Only England's *Punch* could manage a smile and dub the movement, "Sidneywebbicalism," a clever if not very accurate pun.) By the beginning of World War I, the IWW's syndicalistic character was generally accepted. When the IWW was prosecuted during the World War, the tool of repression on the state level was the "criminal syndicalism" law.

Terms such as "syndicalism," names given to systems of thought, have dubious value outside the field of semantics. In the case of the Wobblies and syndicalism, the identification of the two has served to obscure historical perception of the IWW. Indeed, if the IWW had had anything to do with it, the label would never have been fixed, for the union rarely acknowledged the term.[2] Wobblies referred to themselves as revolutionary industrial unionists or industrial unionists or, simply, industrialists. They often explicitly denied, sometimes with vehemence, any relationship with what they considered an essentially European movement.

In January, 1913, for instance, a Wobbly partisan called syndicalism "the name that is most widely used by [the IWW's] enemies." The Wobblies themselves had few kind words for the European syndicalist leaders. To them, Ferdinand Pelloutier was "the anarchist," Georges Sorel, "the monarchist apologist for violence," Hubert Lagardelle was an "anti-democrat," and the Italian Arturo Labriola, "the conservative in politics and revolutionist in labor unionism." The IWW was hostile to all these attitudes. A pro-Wobbly writer noted that the use of the term syndicalism by "bourgeois journalists and magazine writers" when speaking of the IWW, "only leads to confusion." [3]

The point is emphasized in a sympathetic Wobbly review of John Graham Brooks's *American Syndicalism: The IWW*. Although clearly gratified at attracting attention, the IWW reviewer says that Brooks's choice of title is "mistaken" and that Brooks "agrees with many ill-informed socialists" in confusing the IWW "with the European Syndicalist movement." Thirty years later, a once-prominent Wobbly would make the same comment about Paul F. Brissenden's classic history of the movement: "He made the IWW too syndicalist." [4]

The IWW's official word on the semantic wrangle was summed up in a pamphlet published by the Chicago office. In the United States the word syndicalism had been used so incorrectly so often as to mean virtually nothing. "Phrase-mongering apologists for the capitalist system" sought to crush the IWW. "To create a prejudice against it, they called it an importation—syndicalism from Europe." [5]

The IWW had some reason for its annoyance. John Spargo, a scathing critic who was partly responsible for attaching the tag to the IWW in his *Syndicalism, Industrial Unionism, and Socialism,* persisted in calling the Wobblies syndicalists while he admitted that if American "syndicalists" were consistent, they would not act as they did. Both Spargo and John Boyle, the author of an uninformed smear of the IWW, noted that syndicalist literature in English was quite rare. Presumably the "bums" who they said composed the IWW read Sorel, Lagardelle, and Labriola in the original French and Italian. Both authors wrote with a polemical purpose. Spargo, a socialist, wrote his book during a party factional struggle when most of his adversaries were Wobblies or IWW sympathizers. Boyle was a former private secretary to President William McKinley.

He wrote his book originally as an attack on the IWW for the
Cincinnati Enquirer after the Wobblies had led a strike among
Akron rubber industry workers. Disingenuously he revealed
his ignorance of the subject when he lamented to his readers
that he could not find a definition of syndicalism in "the largest dictionary or most comprehensive encyclopedia—not even
in the latest Webster or the last edition of the *Encyclopaedia
Britannica.*" [6]

But Spargo and Boyle had their way. The Wobblies were
ignored when they insisted that "the IWW is not a by-product
of the syndicalist movement." Also ignored were those syndicalists who sought not to be identified with the IWW. Tom
Mann, a syndicalist organizer in Australia and England,
avowed fiercely that he was a syndicalist "as distinct from the
IWW." He urged that the IWW dissolve itself in favor of the
AFL so that true "Syndicalist ideas and methods" might be
expounded and propagated. Wobbly leader Bill Haywood responded sharply by observing that "when Mann presents the
theory of syndicalism and advocates syndicalism . . . he finds
no audience among industrial unionists." [7]

William Z. Foster was another. On his road from populism
to communism, Foster joined the IWW in 1909. An intense
student of radical unionism, Foster traveled to Europe where
he hoped to investigate Continental movements. In France
he lived and worked with the leaders of the *Confédération
Générale du Travail* and was converted to syndicalism. Un-
aware of Foster's new persuasion, the secretary-treasurer of the
IWW cabled Foster and requested him to represent the IWW
at the International Trade Union Secretariat to be held at
Budapest in August, 1911. At the meeting, Foster voted a
straight syndicalist line, echoing the *CGT* on virtually every
issue. This led many observers to assume that the IWW was

merely an extension of the French movement. In fact, Foster's actions represented only himself and proved quite embarrassing to the IWW. Two years later, when it was suggested that the IWW send a delegate to a London congress dominated by syndicalists, several members of the Wobbly executive board reminded the members of the unpleasant experience with Foster. One noted that "we had a representative in Europe once before and what was the result of it? The IWW was simply made a laughingstock of all over the country." The IWW sent no delegate to the 1913 conference.[8]

Indeed, the Wobbly leaders knew that Foster was anxious to transform the IWW into a syndicalist organization when he returned to the United States in 1911. William D. Haywood had met Foster in Paris and observed that Foster was "very much imbued with the idea of syndicalism which he thought should be introduced into America." Neither Haywood nor the other Wobbly leaders were interested. They rejected Foster's syndicalist proposals (chiefly, decentralization and the ending of IWW dual unionism) and Foster quit the IWW. A former Wobbly remembered some years later that "Foster's anarcho-syndicalism lost out. His proposals were rejected in toto." Foster founded a true syndicalist organization, the Syndicalist League of North America, which hobbled along insignificantly for a few years. Only a few anarchists followed him out of the IWW.[9]

The SLNA's chief activity turned out to be the publication of several newspapers filled with anti-IWW, pro-AFL screeds. They damned the IWW as being "democratic and statist" and of "Socialist origin and taint." *The Agitator,* an anarchist paper that had briefly supported the IWW before bolting along with Foster, bemoaned the fact that "the IWW should oppose the introduction of syndicalism into this country, as it is doing." [10]

At about the same time as Foster's secession, Emma Goldman, Alexander Berkman, and some other anarchists attempted to found their own syndicalist group. A Manifesto dated September 30, 1912, and signed by Goldman, Berkman, Margaret Sanger, Hippolyte Havel, and other New York anarchists, proposed the establishment of a Syndicalist League. Their program was quite similar to that of the French *CGT*, but nothing came of it. [11]

In a word, neither the Wobblies nor their syndicalist rivals considered themselves perfect comrades. [12] But why all the fuss? If, indeed, some who used the label were enemies of the IWW others were decidedly not. In fact, as historian Philip S. Foner has pointed out, Wobblies and syndicalists had a great deal in common:

> Both agreed that capitalism must be destroyed and with it the political state must be overthrown; that these ends could only be accomplished by the working class itself; that these goals could not be obtained through political action but only as a result of the direct action of the workers; that society was to be reconstructed by the workers and economic exploitation thereby abolished, and that in the new society, the unions of the workers would own and manage all industries, regulate consumption, and administer the general social interests. [13]

But this tells only part of the story. Their many similarities duly recognized, the Wobblies and the syndicalists differed in particulars quite as fundamental as their similarities: the question of craft versus industrial union structure; the question of dual unionism versus "boring from within"; the question of power and democracy within the union; and the question of political action.

If a Wobbly were asked the name of his philosophy of labor, he would probably answer, "industrial unionism." The fulcrum on which Wobbly discontent with the AFL turned was the old Federation's unequivocal opposition to the organization of workers along industrial lines. To the IWW, craft organization was obsolete and ineffective as unionism. For syndicalists, while many in theory admitted the superiority of industrial organization in well-developed industry, the question of organizational structure seemed not of prime importance. Most European syndicalists accepted the craft organizations they captured as satisfactory facts of life.

In addition to their disillusionment with Gompers' conservatism, a commitment to industrial organization was the single tenuous bond that unified the disparate elements at the convention founding the IWW. All agreed with the clause in the January, 1905, Manifesto which declared that "craft divisions [in unions] foster political ignorance among the workers, thus dividing their class at the ballot box, as well as in the shop, mine and factory." [14] Craft organizations had been rendered obsolete as an effective tool when capitalist organization moved irrevocably toward integration and the industrialization process destroyed what few skills or crafts remained. The famous Preamble stated the case quite succinctly:

> The rapid gathering of wealth and the centering of the management of industries into fewer and fewer hands make the trade unions unable to cope with the ever-growing power of the employing class, because the trade unions foster a state of things which allows one set of workers to be pitted against another set of workers in the same industry, thereby helping defeat one another in wage wars.[15]

An American radical fixture, Oscar Ameringer, described the disillusion with craft unionism in satiric terms for an IWW journal. As far as Ameringer was concerned, the craft unionist was a scab, as bad as the Pinkerton or the strikebreaker. For the craft union member will take "a pattern from a scab patternmaker, cast it in a union mold, hand the casting to as lousy a scab as ever walked in shoe leather, and then proudly produce a paid-up union card in testimony of his unionism." He was in such a position, Ameringer continued, because he belonged to a craft union but was employed in a factory where his craft was no longer relevant. The craft union was ineffective in dealing with the employer at strike time because only the members of that craft walked out. While the striker pickets the gate, a host of other workers nonchalantly cross the line. "Why are they not molested? Oh! They're union men, belonging to a different craft than the one on strike. Instead of brickbats and insults it's 'Hello, John; hello, Jim; howdy, Jack' and other expressions of good fellowship." [16] To the Wobblies, whose whole philosophy would later be distilled into the word, "solidarity," this AFL-fostered situation was ludicrous and reprehensible. Excepting the IWW's revolutionary end, the union structure which they outlined was indistinguishable from the industrial organization espoused by the Congress on Industrial Organizations two decades later. In fact, the organizational aspect of the dispute between the IWW and the AFL is the same controversy which resulted in the secession of the CIO from the AFL late in 1936.

Both IWW and CIO taught that in order to be effective, union organization must parallel the organization of the employer's industry. The employer sees his factory or industry as a whole, not as a collection of autonomous crafts. Unless the union can call a whole factory, or better, an entire industry out of work, it is at a serious bargaining disadvantage vis-à-vis the employer. The CIO, of course, accepted the traditional Gompers' philosophy that the goal was "more" for the workers within the system. Herein the IWW demurred. While the IWW's industrial unions would certainly work for a better life here and now, the Wobblies also visualized the end of capitalist society by means of a final general strike. The industrial union would then serve its ultimate function: the unions would became the governing bodies of the industrial democracy.

Briefly, this was the philosophy of industrial unionism. In practice, it was a matter of organizational structure: unions organized by factory instead of by craft. But the matter of organization was of great importance. With far less convincing reasons than he offered for his antiradicalism, Samuel Gompers unequivocally opposed industrial organization. He summoned all his invective, although little convincing argument, in condemning the "industrialists." Shortly before the founding of the IWW, Gompers told an AFL convention in which a large minority was interested in industrial organization that "the attempt to force the trade unions into what has been termed industrial organization is perversive of the history of the labor movement, runs counter to the best conceptions of the toilers' interests now, and is sure to lead to the confusion which precedes dissolution and disruption." [17] Actually, it was partly Gompers' refusal to consider even the smallest concession to the industrialists which resulted in the 1905 disruption of the labor movement. In view of the fact that the founders of the IWW had little else in common, it is possible that had the AFL not been so hostile to industrial organization, there never would have been an IWW.

Gompers remained adamant. In 1914, moderate socialists

repudiated the IWW in favor of supporting the Socialist and industrial unionist minority within the AFL. Once again in that year, the AFL refused to endorse industrial organization although by doing so Gompers might have been able to destroy his enemies in the IWW.[18] The craft unionists remained in control of the AFL even after Gompers' death and they remained inflexible until 1935 and even after.

Industrial organization was the keystone of the IWW and distinguished the American union from the European syndicalists. While European syndicalism was not theoretically hostile to industrial organization, the syndicalists had emerged from existing unions and remained reasonably content with the old form of organization.

The French syndicalists were in one sense wedded to the preservation of the craft structure. During the power struggles within the *CGT*, from which the syndicalists emerged triumphant, the conservative or "yellow" syndicates favored a system of proportional representation at *CGT* meetings whereby delegates would have voting strength according to how many union members they represented. The syndicalists, in large measure representing the relatively small skilled craft unions, opposed that reform in favor of one vote per craft; they had captured the *CGT* partly because of their overrepresentation. "The autonomy of groups is held to be a principle," Ramsay MacDonald observed of the French.[19] It was a position almost identical to Gompers' passion for the autonomy of crafts in designing their own destinies. One historical analyst, in fact, has noted with some justice that the AFL represented a sort of "conservative syndicalism." [20]

The development of French syndicalism derived from French national and industrial development just as the IWW's development derived from the national and industrial situation in the United States. By the turn of the twentieth century, France was far less industrialized than the United States, and the trend toward industrial consolidation, so familiar in the United States, was as yet hardly visible in France. Relatively, crafts were still of considerable importance in French industry so that Wobbly claims of craft structure obsolescence were not as applicable in France. Furthermore, in the United States, revolutionary industrial unionism appealed almost entirely to unorganized unskilled workers; in France, the anchor of the syndicalist movement was in the anarchistically inclined craft unions of skilled workers. It was not until 1906, after the founding of the IWW, that the syndicalist *CGT* picked up the ideas of industrial structure and then their concession was only partial. At the *CGT* Congress at Amiens, it was decreed that only industrial unions could enter the *CGT* in the future but craft unions already members could remain without alteration or penalty.[21]

Italy was even less advanced industrially than France, and syndicalism was relatively less successful in Italy. The Italians showed little interest in the issue of craft versus industrial organization, so crucial in the United States, and accepted support wherever they found it. To quote a recent historian of the Italian labor movement, "enthusiasm was more important than organization." [22]

Tom Mann in England was opposed to Wobbly-like dual unionism and an advocate of "boring from within." That meant boring from within already existent unions, whether craft or industrial. In theory, Mann was committed to industrial organization (largely because of IWW influence on his thought) but he did not think the issue of telling importance.[23] Haywood criticized Mann for confusing a "federation of federations," patterned after the French *Bourses du Tra-*

vail, with the idea of industrial organization.[24] The Australian movement, although strongly influenced by the IWW, did not emphasize industrial unionism to the exclusion or destruction of the old craft organizations.[25]

William Z. Foster stated that the chief difference between his Syndicalist League of North America and the IWW was the question of dual unionism. That is, Foster advocated dissolution of the IWW and capture of the AFL. But, to reject dual unionism meant to accept, at least momentarily, the craft organization of the AFL.[26] It was this, more than anything, which accounted for the IWW's perfunctory rejection of Foster's syndicalism.

While it was related to the question of structure, the question of dual unionism as opposed to "boring from within" the established conservative unions, was chiefly a problem of method. "Dual unionism" plagued the American labor movement years before the IWW was founded, and it survived long after the IWW was dead as an effective organization. While the question was less obvious than political action as a public issue of contention between the SPA conservatives and the IWW, it played a much more significant role in determining the critical relationship and eventual split between the two organizations.

"Dual unionism" is competitive unionism, two or more unions vying for the allegiance and organization of a certain group of workers. It can be seriously questioned whether the IWW was really a "dual" union. To be sure, a relatively vital AFL already existed when the IWW was founded in 1905. But the Wobblies avowed that they were not interested in seducing AFL locals away from the parent organization. Rather, the IWW was designed to "organize the unorganized," the unskilled in whom the AFL professed a necessary indifference.

Haywood stated at the opening convention that "I do not care a snap of my fingers whether or not the skilled workers join the industrial movement at this time. We are going down into the gutter to get at the mass of workers and bring them up to a decent plane of living." [27] The IWW did not discourage the few disgruntled AFL locals that deserted the old movement for the new and actively courted others. But, after a few years, especially when Haywood's influence increased, the IWW showed little interest in urging AFL unions to reaffiliate. In this light, the IWW would best be defined as "supplementary" rather than "dual"; the union sought out the workers that the AFL ignored.

Nevertheless, the IWW was a rival simply in that it was separate from the AFL. Many moderate socialists and most nonsocialist unionists viewed it as a competitor of the AFL and, therefore, a dual union. Gompers, as one very important example, did not accept the IWW's avowed role of "supplementary" union. To Gompers, the IWW was dual unionism pure and simple. For the man who had been with the AFL since its birth and who was largely responsible for its growth to over a million members in 1905, any other labor organization was an abomination.

It was the unabashed radicalism of the IWW which most alarmed Gompers in 1905 but it was dual unionism which he emphasized in his attacks. That was the theme of Gompers' attack in March, 1905, when he lashed back at the January Manifesto. "The Socialists have called another convention to smash the American trade union movement," Gompers wrote. "This is the sixth 'concentrated effort' in this direction in the past decade." Later in the same editorial he sighed that it was just as well that the convention be held as it would show true unionists who their enemies were all at once.[28] In August, commenting on the convention, Gompers directed his sharpest barbs at the "colossal nerve" of the convention that styled itself the "Industrial Workers of the World." Historians, he noted, would record the Chicago movement as vapid and ridiculous and describe the participants as "the most stupendous impossibles the world has yet seen." [29] The attack remarkably resembled a column Gompers had written a decade before about the founding of Daniel De Leon's Socialist Trades and Labor Alliance, in 1905 a component of the IWW. In fact, Gompers mistakenly believed that his old enemy, De Leon, was the chief architect of the new union.[30]

One accusation which Gompers did not make until several years later was that the IWW was a syndicalist organization. By that time, however, he had plenty of company. But the very fact that the IWW was dual unionist indicates that the Wobblies were not syndicalist. To the European syndicalists, dual or rival unions smelled at least as bad as they did to Gompers. The French syndicalists never gave serious thought to establishing a rival to the *CGT*. The movement there emerged among members of the *CGT*, and their design from the beginning involved capturing the confederation, not seceding from it. The French did not even establish an independent syndicalist daily newspaper until as late as 1911; they preferred to capture the already established journals of the *CGT*.[31]

Emerging as a recognizable movement about 1904, the Italian syndicalists too did not form an organization independent of the *Confederazione Generale del Lavoro.* Many of the leaders of the Italian movement came from the Italian Socialist party rather than from the unions as in France.[32] Inasmuch as they were organized, they resembled the Syndicalist League of North America, a propaganda organization, more than the IWW or the French *CGT*.

They were not dual unionists. Like the French, they sought to capture the *CGL*. In April 1909 the Congress of Syndicalist Resistance meeting in Bologna committed itself to this policy of "boring from within." Unlike the French, however, the Italians were unsuccessful and, after a frustrating three and a half years, separated from the *CGL* on November 24, 1912, to form a dual union.[33] Notably, the vote to secede was so close that had the abstentions been recorded against the move, the resolution might not have carried. At any rate, while the Italians belatedly embraced dual unionism, they did so some seven years after the Wobblies. If there is any question of influence, it is the IWW that influenced the Italian syndicalists and not vice versa.

The British movement provides an interesting facet of the question. According to the contemporary analysts of British syndicalism, the first impetus for the movement came from the United States. Ramsay MacDonald wrote when the first stirrings of the new unionism were being felt in England: "for a good many years the literature of the American Industrial Workers of the World had been circulating in this country." He also noted that a speaking tour by Haywood in South Wales in 1910 had aroused much interest.[34]

The leader of the British movement was Tom Mann. Mann first emerged as a figure in the labor movement as early as 1886 when he led a great dockers' strike. Poor health forced him to emigrate to Australia where he was also involved in union activities and was first introduced to IWW ideas. He returned to England in 1910 to spread the gospel of "industrial unionism." In England, Mann crossbred his Wobbly ideas with French syndicalism, which he had begun to study. Although his particular message remained a combination of both experiences, he became more a syndicalist than a Wobbly. By mid-1912 he was committed to "boring from within" and already critical of IWW dualism.[35] In September, he wrote that "if the opposition of the AF of L should make the continued life of the IWW impossible, then there is the remedy by which both the capitalists and the politicians can be defeated, by rejoining the AF of L unions, and taking up the work with the men inside so that a militant minority can expound and propagate the Syndicalist ideas and methods." [36]

The IWW had smiled upon Mann as a rather celebrated convert and received his veiled attack rather badly. Shortly, Mann criticized the IWW more directly. Writing a letter to the anarchistic *Agitator* (which supported William Z. Foster's SLNA), Mann complimented the newspaper which he was pleased to see "was now syndicalist." (The *Agitator* had recently broken with the IWW.) Mann continued: "I am a Syndicalist as opposed to the IWW. I suppose I am correct in understanding the latter to be on principle in antagonism to the existing trade unions and aiming at building up an entirely new Industrial organization." [37] Two years later, Haywood responded to Mann's increasing criticisms of IWW dual unionism. "When Mann presents [the idea of] a federation of federations as a practical progressive step, he finds no audience among industrial unionists who have for years been preparing the ground for a new structure of society" on their own. The IWW was not buying Mann's syndicalist policy of boring from within.[38]

Foster's SLNA, and not the IWW, was Mann's counterpart in the United States. Foster's chief grievance with the IWW was the Wobblies' commitment to a separate union. Conversations with leaders of the *CGT* had convinced Foster that the "syndicalist way" was to dissolve the IWW and affiliate with the AFL. His Syndicalist League, Foster wrote in his autobiography, "in the main . . . followed the general lines of French Syndicalism." [39]

The short life of the SLNA was devoted almost entirely to attacks on the IWW, and the organization enjoyed little success boring from within.

The organization of the IWW was highly centralized. When Father Thomas J. Hagerty graphically charted the organization of the union, he selected as most representative a series of concentric circles. In the center he placed the General Administration and at the center of that, the president.[40] Emanating from the General Administration were large slices of pie, each representing a different department of the union. These contained smaller slices. Thus, the largest, the "Department of Manufactures," included the textile industry, the leather industry, etc. There were also departments of Distribution, Public Service, Mining, and so on. Within the slices, Hagerty listed specific industries which would comprise locals, for example, within the Department of Public Service: Teachers, Librarians, Firemen, Actors, Musicians, Animal Keepers, Chambermaids, Printers, and Telephone Operators. (Policemen were conspicuously absent.) Projected locals in the Department of Foodstuffs were Meat Cutters, Milkers, Packers, Bakers, Brewers, Deliverymen, and so on. While comprehensive, the chart was also quite speculative, considering the small numbers of the IWW, in fact, a pipe dream. Gompers mocked the plan as Father Hagerty's "Wheel of Fortune." [41] The "Wheel" was revised frequently, always toward simplification.

The chief feature of this plan was that it visualized "One Big Union" and that slogan became a rallying cry of the

IWW. It provided a dramatic contrast to the "American Separation of Labor," as Wobblies derisively called the AFL. Industrial unionism, one union for an entire factory or industry, was extended in theory to a single union of all workers. The central administration of the union was the future central government "within the shell of the old society" just as the departments and locals were, "within the shell of the old," the future subordinate governing agencies of the "industrial democracy."

The highly centralized union structure was often challenged from within the IWW, especially by the western wing, but always unsuccessfully before the World War, when external forces not only decentralized but dispersed the movement. In 1914, the Wobblies, chiefly in the West and South, sought a decentralization of power on the grounds that every city and town was the center of some particular agricultural or commercial activity. They proposed that a highly centralized organization was inadequate to meet these facts and that the "One Big Union" should be divided into regions for administrative purposes.[42] Their motion was defeated, and the General Executive Board remained in full control. The decentralists' goals closely resembled the structure of the *CGT*. The French syndicalist opposition to proportional representation was part of their larger opposition to a centralized confederation.[43] Ramsay MacDonald noted the syndicalists' assertion that "the opinion of a small union is likely to be right as that of a large union." [44] Just as important, much of French syndicalist support was rooted in the relatively small local craft unions. A centralized administration might well have hamstrung the local syndicates in their particularistic aims.

One of these aims was the spontaneous, unannounced strike. The syndicalists visualized the strike not as "an unfortunate but finally necessary act of hostility, when all other means have failed" but rather, as "the natural and desirable expression of the enmity of capital and labour." Moreover, following Georges Sorel, the local strike was a taste of the final, glorious catastrophe, the "myth" of the general strike. Tom Mann phrased it accurately when he wrote that "we most certainly favor strikes; we shall always do our best to help strikes to be successful, and shall prepare the way as rapidly as possible for THE GENERAL STRIKE of national proportions." [45]

The IWW favored strikes too; to a considerable degree they too visualized each strike for immediate demands as a rehearsal (and perhaps even the immediate prelude) to the general strike. However, the IWW was not so promiscuous in the use of the weapon, and therein lies the greater significance of the matter. For the Wobblies, there were times when it was wiser not to strike, an inconceivable point of view for the syndicalist. Thus, while the syndicalists favored granting a maximum autonomy to their locals so that they might strike at their own behest with no warning to the enemy, one reason why the IWW favored centralization was so that the General Executive Board, presumably more knowledgeable of overall conditions, could temper hotheads in the locals who might commit the union to a futile and injurious battle.

While the European syndicalists advocated decentralization in order to give the local more freedom of action, they were not democratic by any means. The syndicalists had a singularly dim view of the workers' ability to seek their own best interests. In 1901, a leading syndicalist journal described "the majorities" as "sheep-like, unthinking, . . . they accept the accomplished facts and endure the worst extortions." [46] The syndicalists had a curiously Leninist view of how the mass might be moved: "If it is a question of a strike, an insurrection, or even a simple election, the action of minorities is preponderant. It is the minorities which sow and propagate new ideas, and when the psychological moment has come, goad the inert mass to action." [47]

While in practice the IWW leaders often accepted the principle of manipulation involved in this point of view, they were in theory inalterably opposed to it. The IWW espoused a participatory sort of democracy in which, while authority was centralized, all members shared in that authority. Their rhetoric illustrates a romantic's commitment to the inherent wisdom of the masses. It was a point of pride for the Wobblies to reply to the question, "Who are your leaders?" with the answer, "We are all leaders." Notably, Foster's SLNA damned the IWW for being "democratic" among other things. Foster based his ill-fated group on the syndicalist premise of the militant minority which was "the thinking and acting part of the working class [that] takes the lead." [48] The extent of genuine democracy within the IWW is, of course, a matter difficult and perhaps impossible to determine from the scarce sources available. But, in principle, at least, the IWW differed from the syndicalists on the question. [49]

Ultimately, for both contemporary critics of the IWW and subsequent analysts, the identification of the IWW and the syndicalists returns to the question of political action. It was upon the IWW's ostensible rejection of the ballot that the Socialist party of America disassociated itself from the IWW in 1913 and it was this same "rejection" which a recent historian has called the IWW's "basic error." [50] The judgment that the IWW was antipolitical is the most unfortunate result of the historical identification of Wobblies and syndicalists for the two movements held radically different views on the subject.

Political action may be defined in two ways. In the broad-

est sense it may include all propaganda action: soapbox
speeches, demonstrations, the press, pamphleteering, etc.
Neither the European syndicalists nor the IWW nor, for that
matter, most anarchists, eliminated that sort of agitation. In
the narrower but germane sense, political action means voting,
standing for office, legislation, initiating action through the
courts, or in any way implementing the power of the political
state to advance the interests of the cause, in this case, the
workers.

The syndicalists considered the capitalist state incapable of
meaningful progress and repudiated all such political action.
It was impossible for the working class to utilize institutions
that had been established by the ruling class for the very purpose of suppressing the workers. The only road to socialism
was through the direct action of the workers themselves. For
the syndicalist, the political party was bourgeois by definition
and therefore completely worthless. It was immaterial that
certain parties called themselves "Socialist" or "Labor."

The IWW disdained politics on similar grounds. Like the
syndicalists, the Wobblies did not believe that Socialism could
be established through political action. Like the syndicalists,
the IWW thought it absurd to believe that the workers could
"vote socialism in." As Jack London, something of a Wobbly
himself, wrote: "History shows that no master class is ever
willing to let go without a quarrel. The capitalists own the
government, the armies, and the militia. Don't you think capitalists will use these institutions to keep themselves in
power?" [51]

As an organization, the IWW would not participate in political action at all. At the 1908 convention, Daniel De Leon
and the Socialist Labor party Wobblies were expelled, and a
reference to political action in the Preamble was deleted be-

cause of well-founded fears that De Leon sought to convert the IWW into a wing of the SLP. But this was not an anti-political action. *Solidarity*, an official IWW journal, pointed out that the IWW kept politics out of the union in order to avoid control by political parties. The union was not anti-political but, rather, nonpolitical.[52]

While it rejected control by political parties, the IWW reserved an important, albeit secondary, role for political action in their quest for "industrial democracy." They viewed the Socialist party as fulfilling several functions. First, the Socialist party could prevent legislation adverse to the working class and prevent the use of the police and military against strikers. As the Wobblies phrased it, Socialist politicians would withhold the policeman's club. According to a pro-Wobbly writer, the political party's major job was "to hamper the ruling class in the war it will be waging on the revolutionary unions." [53] From the Wobbly point of view that the union was the agency of revolution, this was a *positive* function.

The political party's second function was *negative*, namely, to exhort reform legislation from the capitalist-owned municipalities, states, and perhaps even the federal government. The IWW approved heartily of minimum wage laws, codes prohibiting the use of child labor, tenement legislation, and any concessions from the capitalists that might ameliorate the workers' position. They disagreed completely with those radicals, including the syndicalists, who subscribed to the dictum, "the worse the better," because that meant the revolution was imminent. The Wobblies approved any and all immediate gains just as long as the workers did not view "crumbs" as the entire loaf.[54]

Third, the political party was invaluable as an educational agency. Through its political campaigns the party could transmit sound knowledge to the workers and educate them in the principles of revolutionary industrial unionism. All the better if the Socialists won their elections; their victories would draw the curiosity of the workers.[55] It was important, however, that socialist politicians not be deluded into thinking that they were accomplishing the revolution through holding office.

Fourth, the Socialist party's vote could serve the IWW as a sort of popularity poll, a register of the support the workers could expect to get in the event of a strike or demonstration. The IWW subscribed to the old American Labor Union's view that the political party's vote was merely "public expression" so far as revolution was concerned.[56]

Fifth, when capitalism finally crumbled as a result of the general strike, the political Socialists would help the political state destroy itself. (In that Socialist electoral success would increase as the revolution neared, this would be an easy but important task.) At a speech in Cooper Union in 1912, Haywood emphasized that "with the success of socialism practically all the political offices now in existence will be put out of business," and socialist politicians would help in the process.[57]

The crux of the matter was that socialism could be established only by the revolutionary union; political action *alone* was impotent and ludicrous. Haywood had continued in his Cooper Union speech: "I want to say . . . that while a member of the Socialist party and a believer in political action, it is decidedly better in my opinion to be able to elect the superintendent in some branch of industry than to elect a congressman to the United States Congress." [58] Another Wobbly described the Wobblies' limited concept of political action more specifically: "I travelled forty miles to vote for Debs and Hanford last election and wasn't sure I could vote when I got there. But I voted. So, I am not against political action. But it doesn't always go far enough." [59] Wobbly words and actions stating their acceptance of political action and even cooperation with the Socialist party are so many and obvious that it is almost incredible that the IWW's critics should have been so successful in labeling the movement syndicalist.

Big Bill Haywood, whose influence within the IWW grew steadily after 1912, was the union's chief advocate of cooperation with the Socialist party. His socialist politics dated back to his youth. As he rose from the ranks to leadership in his union, the Western Federation of Miners (the buttress of the SPA in the Mountain States), he rose to prominence in the Socialist party as well. In 1904, he wrote a pamphlet for Debs's presidential campaign called, "The Wolf," in which he urged voting Socialist as the way to eliminate "rascally government, poverty and crime" and the way to achieve collective ownership of the nation's resources. He modified this exalted concept of political action within a few years but he never abandoned the principle itself. In 1906, while awaiting trial for the murder of ex-Governor Frank Steunenburg of Idaho, Haywood was nominated for Governor of Colorado on the Socialist ticket. He polled 16,000 votes as opposed to only some 2,000 which the party had drawn two years before.[60]

In 1908, a cause célèbre after his acquittal in the Steunenburg case, Haywood campaigned for Debs and rode the "Red Special," the SPA campaign train, for part of its journey. He spoke on Debs's behalf at the closing rally at Terre Haute. In fact, there is some evidence that some of Haywood's friends had sought to nominate him as SPA candidate for President or Vice-President in 1908, hardly the role for an antipolitical ideologue. Ironically, reformist socialists such as Morris Hillquit, who, four years later, would be damning Haywood's antipoliticalism, were more concerned in 1908 that Haywood might actively seek a place on the national ticket. During a lecture tour in 1910 throughout Europe, when some critics said that Haywood fell under the syndicalist spell, he consistently expressed nonsyndicalist points of view. For example, when he thanked his audiences for the working class solidarity to which he attributed his acquittal in a celebrated trial in 1907, he asked his listeners "to do for yourself what you have done for me," namely, "to organize politically as well as industrially." That speech was one of Haywood's last in Europe and there is no evidence that he was affected by any syndicalists he might have met on the tour.[61]

Frank Bohn, with Haywood the coarchitect of the IWW's industrial unionist policy, not only approved political action himself, he was harshly critical of the few "antipolitical fanatics" within the IWW. Vincent St. John, Haywood's predecessor as secretary-treasurer of the IWW, was cooler than most to the usefulness of political action. Nevertheless, his chief criticisms were aimed at those Wobblies and socialists who advocated affiliation of union and party. While he maintained unequivocally that the IWW would never endorse any political party, he made it clear that "neither will the IWW carry on a propaganda against political action." He acknowledged the usefulness of the party. To those Wobblies who felt that the workers should be united in a party as well as the union, he added, "we say, dig in and do so."[62]

Thomas J. Hagerty was one of the chief targets for those who called the IWW syndicalist and antipolitical. It was Hagerty who authored the sardonic statement that "dropping pieces of paper into a hole in a box never did achieve emancipation for the working class and it never will." The chance statement was quoted out of all proportion to its significance;

Wobblies rarely repeated it, only the IWW's enemies. Moreover, the critics completely ignored other Hagerty statements
in quite a different vein. The pages of the *Voice of Labor*,
which Hagerty edited during the months before the IWW's
first convention, were preoccupied with the question of political action, and Hagerty several times allowed that such action
had some value to the class struggle. Furthermore, as the first
speaker at the ratification session of the first IWW convention, Hagerty specifically quoted the "political action" clause
of the Preamble with no embarrassment and he stamped his
approval on the clause. Finally, to emphasize Hagerty is to
ignore the fact that while he was an important figure at the
founding convention, he drifted away from the IWW immediately and played no part whatsoever in the union's subsequent development.[63]

Dual support of both the IWW and the Socialist party per-
meated the lowest Wobbly ranks. Eugene V. Debs, William
English Walling, and other sympathetic analysts of the IWW
were confident that most Wobblies voted SPA. In 1906, the
entire Socialist ticket in Colorado consisted of Wobblies and
the major SPA victory in the city of Butte, Montana, in April
1911 was generally attributed to mass IWW support.[64] In fact,
when the Socialist party repudiated Haywood in 1913, the disgruntled Butte Wobblies withheld their votes from the "sewer
socialist" administration, and the Montana party fell out of
power and quickly disintegrated.

There must have been many Wobblies and IWW partisans
in the party in 1910 for, in the party's election for delegates to
the International Socialist Congress, Haywood's vote exceeded
that of such well-known moderate socialists as the New York
City leader, Morris Hillquit; the publisher, Gaylord Wilshire;
John Spargo, Robert Hunter, May Wood Simons, and ex-

Wobbly, Ernest Untermann. Haywood's vote was narrowly exceeded only by that of the Milwaukee party boss, Victor Berger.[65]

The Wobbly-led Lawrence strike, often interpreted as a syndicalist revolution, actually aided the SPA in the state of Massachusetts until the party repudiated the IWW. A social gospel Protestant minister and former SPA gubernatorial candidate called upon socialists to recognize that the IWW and SPA support of the IWW was the best means toward gaining electoral success in the state.[66] The Paterson silk-weavers' general strike of 1913 had much the same effect. Before the Wobbly-led strike, the highest Socialist vote ever recorded in Paterson was 1,650. At the municipal election of November 1913 the SPA candidate for mayor received 5,155 votes, only some 2,000 fewer than the victorious Republican-Progressive fusion candidate. In adjoining boroughs, the Socialists also gained. The SPA vote in Passaic increased by 500, Haledon voted Socialist, and North Haledon elected three Socialists to the borough council. The increased vote came from silk weavers organized by the IWW and other strike sympathizers. Wobblies maintained that if the AFL members in Paterson had voted as solidly Socialist as the IWW's, the SPA would have won the city. Pat Quinlan, one of the IWW-SPA leaders in Paterson, concluded that "the silk workers had learned the lesson of class solidarity and the necessity of carrying that solidarity into the political field." [67]

Even the western wing of the IWW, which was less well disposed to political action than the eastern, exhibited political leanings in the early years of the movement. Covington Hall, later dubbed an anarchist, described how the IWW exerted its political influence in Louisiana:

As long as the *Lumberjack* [on IWW paper] was published in Louisiana it defeated every politician known to be an enemy of the workers and the farmers. We held strictly to the rule of the IWW not to endorse any candidate for public office; if we did not want a candidate elected, we hammered him week in and out in the paper as an "enemy of labor," leaving it to the people to support and vote for his opponent as they saw fit. This was so effective that the politicians of middle and western Louisiana came to fear the *Lumberjack* as the devil fears holy water, saying: "I would rather have the opposition of the entire daily press of the State than of that damn sheet." [68]

Despite the allegations of the IWW's enemies, then, neither the leaders nor the rank and file were antipolitical. Nor was the organization antipolitical in its official statements. Much has been made of the fact that the "political clause" of the 1905 Preamble was deleted in 1908. The critics who emphasize the 1908 action, however, do not mention an equally significant action by the membership at the 1911 convention. It was proposed that an antipolitical clause be added to the Preamble. The clause read: "Realizing the futility of political action, and recognizing the absolute necessity of the industrial union, we unite under the following constitution." The amendment was voted down without discussion.[69]

NOTES

1. To cite a few: James Boyle, *The Minimum Wage and Syndicalism* (Cincinnati: Stewart & Kidd Co., 1913); Paul F. Brissenden, *The Launching of the Industrial Workers of the World* (Berkeley: University of California Press, 1913); Justus Ebert, *The Trial of a New Society* (Cleveland: IWW Publishing Bureau, 1913); Arthur D. Lewis, *Syndicalism and*

the General Strike (London: T. F. Unwin, 1912); John Spargo, *Syndicalism, Industrial Unionism, and Socialism* (New York: B. W. Huebsch, 1913); Andre Tridon, *The New Unionism* (New York: B. W. Huebsch, 1913); William E. Walling, *Socialism as It Is: A Survey of the World-Wide Revolutionary Movement* (New York: Macmillan Co., 1918).

2. Eldridge Foster Dowell, *A History of Criminal Syndicalism Legislation in the United States* (Baltimore: Johns Hopkins Press, 1939), p. 27. The occasional Wobbly recognition of kinship inevitably included an emphasis of differences. For a somewhat different view, see Philip S. Foner, *History of the Labor Movement in the United States* (New York: International Publishing Co., 1965) 4, *The Industrial Workers of the World, 1905–1917*, 158 (hereafter cited as *The IWW*).

3. William E. Walling, "Industrial or Revolutionary Unionism," *New Review* 1 (January 11, 1913): 46; idem, "Industrialism versus Syndicalism," *International Socialist Review* 14 (August, 1913): 666 (hereafter cited as *ISR*).

4. "New Books," *ISR* 14 (August, 1913): 119; Ralph Chaplin, interview with Donald M. Barnes, April 7, 1959, quoted in Donald M. Barnes, "The Ideology of the Industrial Workers of the World" (Ph.D. diss., Washington State University, 1962).

5. "Historical Catechism of American Unionism," IWW pamphlet (Chicago, n.d.); see also William D. Haywood, *Bill Haywood's Book: The Autobiography of William D. Haywood* (New York: International Publishers, 1929), p. 237; *The Agitator* (Lakebay, Washington), June 15, 1912. For a final and feeble Wobbly disclaimer of syndicalism, see "The IWW Reply to the Red Trade Union International," IWW pamphlet (Chicago, 1922).

6. Boyle, *Minimum Wage and Syndicalism*, pp. 87, 134; Spargo, *Syndicalism*, pp. 37, 242.

7. Tom Mann, letter, *The Agitator*, September 15, 1912; editorial, *The Syndicalist* (London), September, 1912; William D. Haywood, "An Appeal for Industrial Solidarity," *ISR* 14 (March, 1914): 544.

8. Harvey O'Connor, *Revolution in Seattle* (New York: Monthly Review Press, 1964), p. 16; William Z. Foster, *From Bryan to Stalin* (London: Lawrence & Wishart, 1937), pp. 49, 51; *Stenographic Report of the Eighth Annual Convention of the IWW* (Cleveland, 1913), p. 13; Vincent St. John to Guy Bowman, August 9, 1913, London, Labadie Collection.

9. Haywood, *Bill Haywood's Book*, p. 237; Ralph Chaplin, *Wobbly: The Rough and Tumble Story of an American Radical* (Chicago: University of Chicago Press, 1948), p. 137; Elizabeth Gurley Flynn, *I Speak My Own Piece: Autobiography of the Rebel Girl* (New York: International Publishing Co., 1955), p. 161.

10. *The Agitator*, October 15, 1912; see also William Z. Foster, *History of the Communist Party in the United States* (New York: International Publishers, 1952), pp. 117–118; G. D. H. Cole, *World of Labour* (London:) p. 156. An excellent collection of SLNA clippings is included in the Agnes

Inglis scrapbook in the Labadie Collection of the University of Michigan Library.

11. Foster, *From Bryan to Stalin*, p. 59.

12. Nor did a few nonpartisans. See Mary B. Sumner, "Parting of the Ways in American Socialism," *The Survey* 29 (February 1, 1913): 626; "American Economists on Syndicalism," *New Review* 2 (May, 1914): 308. At least one contemporary analyst examined the crucial difference between industrial unionism and syndicalism in detail. Louis Fraina (better known later as Lewis Corey) was favorable to the IWW and feared that it was in danger of becoming syndicalist. Fortunately, according to Fraina, that had not happened by mid-1913. He wrote that it was regrettable that syndicalism had been adopted by some as "a synonym for Revolutionary Unionism" because, while syndicalism was anarchistic and "opposed to the Socialist philosophy . . . Industrial Unionism [the IWW] is the application of Socialist principles to economic organization." Fraina saw syndicalism as arising primarily "as a protest against political inefficiency and cowardice" while the IWW "arose primarily as a recognition of the vast power inherent in the industrial groups into which the mechanism of centralized capitalist production marshals the workers." "Syndicalism and Industrial Unionism," *ISR* 14 (July, 1913): 25, 28.

13. Foner, *The IWW*, p. 159.

14. "Manifesto," *Proceedings of the First Convention of the IWW* (Chicago: IWW Publishing Bureau, 1905). The "Manifesto" is also published in Joyce Kornbluh, *Rebel Voices: An IWW Anthology* (Ann Arbor: University of Michigan Press, 1964), pp. 7–9.

15. "Preamble," *Proceedings of the First Convention*. The Wobblies were proud enough of their succinct and literary declaration of principle to print it in virtually every one of their pamphlets, flyers, and books. This clause appears in both the 1905 and 1908 versions with only a few minor variations. For an easily accessible copy of the Preamble, see Kornbluh, *Rebel Voices*, pp. 12–13.

16. Oscar Ameringer, "Union Scabs," *Industrial Union Bulletin*, March 14, 1908.

17. *National Proceedings of the AFL, 1904* (Washington, D.C.: AFL Printing Office, 1904) p. 353; *AFL Yearbook*, 1916 (Washington, D.C.: AFL Printing Office, 1916), p. 247.

18. *National Proceedings of the AFL, 1914* (Washington, D.C.: AFL Printing Office, 1916), p. 18.

19. James Ramsay MacDonald, *Syndicalism* (Chicago: Open Court Publishing Co., 1913), p. 45.

20. James A. Estey, *Revolutionary Syndicalism* (London: P. S. King & Son, 1913), p. 45. The IWW was always committed to the principle of proportional representation in policy matters. See Will Herberg, "American Marxist Political Theory," in *Socialism and American Life*, 1, ed. Donald G. Egbert and Stow Persons, Princeton Studies in American Civilization, vol. 4 (Princeton, N.J.: Princeton University Press, 1952), 491.

21. Emile Pouget, *La Confederation Generale du Travail* (Paris: M. Riviere et Cie., [1910]), p. 19; Robert Hunter, *Violence and the Labor Movement* (New York: Macmillan Co., 1919), p. 247.

22. Daniel L. Horowitz, *Italian Labor Movement* (Cambridge: Harvard University Press, 1963), p. 79.

23. In Mann's synopsis of his views quoted in John Hunter Harley, *Syndicalism* (London: T. C. & E. C. Jack, 1912), pp. 44–45, he states that it is necessary "for every worker to belong to a union, and for every union to unite with every other union in the same industry," but nothing is said of the cardinal Wobbly ideal of "One Big Union."

24. Haywood, "An Appeal for Industrial Solidarity," p. 544. Mann's letter to the *Agitator*, September 15, 1912, criticized IWW opposition to "existing trade unions," which means, of course, the AFL.

25. Ken Walker, "Australia," in Walter Galenson, *Comparative Labor Movements* (New York: Russell & Russell, 1952), p. 186.

26. Foster, *History of the Communist Party*, pp. 117–118.

27. *Proceedings of the First Convention*, pp. 474–476.

28. *American Federationist* 12 (March, 1905): 139, 141.

29. *Ibid.*, 12 (August, 1905): 515–516.

30. *Ibid.*, 3 (April, 1896): 33.

31. Emile Pataud and Emile Pouget, *Syndicalism and the Cooperative Commonwealth: How We Shall Bring About the Revolution*, trans. C. and F. Charles (Oxford: New International Publishing Co., 1913); Walling, *Socialism as It Is*, p. 366.

32. Horowitz, *Italian Labor*, pp. 52–53.

33. Tridon, *New Unionism*, pp. 153, 155.

34. MacDonald, *Syndicalism*, pp. 42–43.

35. Walling, *Socialism as It Is*, p. 357.

36. Editorial, *The Syndicalist* (London), September, 1912.

37. *The Agitator*, September 15, 1912.

38. Haywood, "An Appeal for Industrial Solidarity," p. 544.

39. Foster, *From Bryan to Stalin*, p. 60; *History of the Communist Party*, pp. 117–118.

40. In 1906, the office of president was abolished in favor of a multi-member General Executive Board. The secretary-treasurer was then chief executive for all practical purposes.

41. Father Hagerty's original "Wheel of Fortune" is reproduced in Kornbluh, *Rebel Voices*, p. 10.

42. Covington Hall, "Labor Struggles in the Deep South," typescript, Labor History Archives, Wayne State University, n.d., p. 232.

43. Estey, *Revolutionary Syndicalism*, p. 45.

44. MacDonald, *Syndicalism*, p. 30.

45. Griffuelhes and Neil, "Les Objectifs," quoted from a translation in Estey, *Revolutionary Syndicalism*, p. 77.

46. *La Voix du Peuple*, May, 1901.

47. *Ibid.*, September, 1901.

48. Quoted in Cole, *World of Labour,* p. 156; see also Foster, *From Bryan to Stalin,* p. 62.

49. For an elaboration of this point, see Joseph R. Conlin, "Wobblies and Syndicalists," *Studies on the Left,* 6 (March–April, 1966), pp. 81–91.

50. Foner, *The IWW,* p. 470.

51. Philip S. Foner, *Jack London: American Rebel* (New York: Citadel Press, 1947), p. 96.

52. *Solidarity,* July 23, 1910. In retrospect, the IWW's point of view can be better understood in view of what seems to be the valid principle most recently articulated by Frank Tannenbaum in his *A Philosophy of Labor* (New York: Alfred A. Knopf, 1951), p. 90. Tannenbaum notes that the "Socialists, like the Communists, have a purpose beyond trade-unionism and the trade-unions must be a tool for the fulfillment of future plans." As a youth, Tannenbaum was a Wobbly, although in an unimportant capacity. Certainly, his membership had little lasting effect on his later views about labor.

53. Walling, "Industrial or Revolutionary Unionism," p. 49; see also idem, "What Is the Matter with the Socialist Party?," *ISR* 10 (November, 1909): 451; Frank Bohn, "The Ballot," *ISR* 10 (June, 1910): 1120.

54. Louis Duchez, "The Strikes in Pennsylvania," *ISR* 10 (September, 1909): 203.

55. Frank Bohn, "The Ballot," p. 1120; Haywood and Bohn, "Industrial Unionism," *ISR* 12 (December, 1911): 368; Walling, "Industrial or Revolutionary Unionism," p. 49.

56. *ALU Journal,* December, 1904; Sumner, "Parting of the Ways," p. 630.

57. Haywood, "Socialism the Hope of the Workers, *ISR* 12 (February, 1912): 426. See also Sumner, "Parting of the Ways," p. 630.

58. Haywood, "Socialism the Hope of the Workers," p. 462.

59. M. B. Butler, letter to *ISR* 11 (November, 1910): 315. See also Chaplin, *Wobbly,* p. 83; *ISR* 12 (July, 1911): 55; Frank Bohn, "Is the I.W.W. to Grow?" *ISR* 12 (July, 1911): 42–44. A Wobbly who was also an anarchist advocated cooperation with the Socialist party for a different and novel reason. He explained his position in a parable: "There are some people in Trenton . . . who have a long journey to go along a road which is difficult and obstructed. Perhaps many robbers are on the road who will stop them. Some are going to Elizabeth, for instance, and some others to New York; the party which is going to New York will certainly join the other party which goes to Elizabeth to help each other along the road, the party for New York explaining to the other party why they do not stop at Elizabeth but go further. Yes, dear comrades, I have joined the Socialist Party because you are going my road. I will walk with you showing you the necessity of running and not stopping." Jules Scarceriaux, *The Demonstrator,* September 4, 1907.

60. Ira Kipnis, *The American Socialist Movement: 1897–1912* (New York: Columbia University Press, 1952), p. 192; *Bill Haywood's Book,* p. 202; *Social Democratic Herald* (Milwaukee), August 11, 1906.

61. *Bill Haywood's Book,* p. 230; Charles Sprague Smith to Morris Hillquit, March 18, 1908, Hillquit Papers, State Historical Society of Wisconsin. The final statement was made at a lecture in People's House, Christiana, Norway ("Haywood in Europe," *ISR* 11 [November, 1910]: 288). Haywood's trial is discussed in detail in Joseph R. Conlin, "The Haywood Case: An Enduring Riddle," *Pacific Northwest Quarterly,* January, 1968, pp. 23–32. For a more extensive account of Haywood's views on political action, see Joseph R. Conlin, *Big Bill Haywood and the Radical Labor Movement* (Syracuse: Syracuse University Press, 1969).

62. Bohn repeated his position repeatedly in the *ISR* ("Is the I.W.W. to Grow?" 12 [July, 1911]: 44); "Fighting Weapons" 15 (October, 1914): 272; "The Failure to Attain Socialist Unity" 15 (October, 1914): 755; "Some Definitions" 12 (May, 1912): 747–749; St. John, "Political Parties and the IWW," IWW leaflet (New Castle, Pa., n.d.), Socialist Party Collection, Duke University Library; *Proceedings of the First Convention,* p. 152.

63. *Proceedings of the First Convention,* p. 569; *Voice of Labor* 3 (March, 1905).

64. *ISR* 12 (September, 1911): 186; Frank Bohn, "Some Definitions," pp. 747–749; Eugene V. Debs, "A Plea for Solidarity," *ISR* 14 (March, 1914): 537; Walling, *Socialism as It Is*; Kipnis, *American Socialist Movement,* p. 197; Jack Keister, "Why the Socialists Won at Butte," *ISR* 11 (June, 1911): 733.

65. *ISR* 11 (July, 1910): 56.

66. Rev. Roland D. Sawyer, "The Socialist Situation in Massachusetts," *New Review* 1 (January 25, 1913): 117–118.

67. Pat Quinlan, "The Paterson Strike and After," *New Review* 2 (January, 1914): 31–32.

68. Covington Hall, "Labor Struggles," pp. 186–187.

69. B. H. Williams, "Sixth IWW Convention," *ISR* 12 (November, 1911): 301.

2

A Conglomeration of Freaks

GEORGE SPEED of the AFL's Seamen's Union commented of the unlikely allies who met at Chicago to form the IWW, that it was "the greatest conglomeration of freaks that ever met in a convention." [1] It was fair enough, if somewhat acerbic an analysis. Revolutionaries, and perhaps especially American radicals, have always seemed more enthusiastic in fighting one another than they have in allying to attack their common enemy. The leaders of the 1905 Wobbly convention had been combatants for years. Members of the Socialist party of America winced at the sometimes violent militance of the Western Federation of Miners, and the Socialists were split among themselves. All of the SPA members and many of the unionists, moreover, had shunned Socialist Laborite Daniel De Leon who, in his turn, was bitter in denouncing the SPA "slowshulists."

Still, they did meet and all did their best to be mannerly. Speech after speech called for the interment of old rivalries. Pleas for unity alternated with maudlin testimonies of past

offenses against the common weal and promises of better behavior in the future. All the convention leaders called wish-
fully for unity during the deliberations. Eugene V. Debs op-
timistically dismissed wide differences "in detail" in view of
the fact that "upon the great vital principle of uniting the
working class upon the economic field in a revolutionary organization recognizing the class struggle," those at the convention were one.[2] Algie Simons, who shortly before the meeting
had aimed some poisoned barbs at De Leon, managed to avoid
the subject during the convention. Bill Haywood, in accepting
the chairmanship of the gathering, wished that at such a convention, "there is or should be no factions, and where you are
all in hearty accord and are working for the same purpose,
there should be no reason for any wranglings or any personali-
ties, and I hope there will be none indulged in." [3] Even Daniel
De Leon sounded like a mellow, conciliatory old grandfather,
a striking example of self-discipline. "During this process of
pounding one another," he said, "we have both learned, and
I hope and believe that this convention will bring together
those who will plant themselves squarely upon the class struggle." [4] And so it went.

But the Brand's Hall meeting ushered in no golden age of
unity on the American left. The pleas for unity evinced a
recognition of disunity as much as anything. Robert F. Hoxie
correctly noted in 1913 that factionalism, not the hopeful chord
of unity expressed in 1905, was "the keynote" of Wobbly history.[5] Almost as soon as the convention had completed its work,
rival groups coalesced to challenge the right of each other not
only to dominance of the young organization but to any voice
in its policies whatsoever. The story of the IWW's first years
is not an account of strikes and progress toward the industrial
democracy but, rather, of debilitating internecine strife, con-

testing factions that, a socialist AFL leader suggested, "would require a Philadelphia lawyer to determine accurately which faction [had] the advantage." [6]

Only one division within the organization derived from ideological considerations. That is, while almost all of the delegates claimed to be socialists, there was also present a small group of anarchists, the remnants of the Chicago group. Lucy Parsons, widow of the Haymarket martyr Albert Parsons, was honored by a prominent seat and spoke several times. But she functioned primarily as platform decoration and had little influence on the proceedings. Her ignominious role characterized the dilemma of the less eminent anarchists: tolerated in attendance, they went all but unheard. Mrs. Parsons sheepishly apologized for employing the term "anarchy" in a speech, and the few avowedly anarchist proposals that reached the floor were summarily rejected. Nevertheless, with the exception of Emma Goldman's *Mother Earth* (which was silent), anarchist journals welcomed the new union. Lucy Parsons' *Liberator* was short-lived, enduring barely long enough to bless the IWW. But Jay Fox's healthier *Demonstrator* devoted a regular department to IWW news and carried a Wobbly "bug." [7]

Why anarchists could approve an organization dominated by socialists is explained by the IWW's strict nonpolitical policy. A clause in the Preamble which became an issue of some moment read:

> Between these two classes a struggle must go on until all the toilers come together on the political, as well as on the industrial field, and take and hold that which they produce by their labor, through an economic organization of the working class without affiliation with any political party.[8]

If the statement explicitly acknowledged the viability of political action, it was nevertheless acceptable to the anarchists inasmuch as it just as explicitly restricted the IWW to direct action without any political function or association.

This "first principle" was no concession to the inconsequential anarchists but, rather, the work of the IWW's "unionists-first"—those who were interested in the construction of an economic organization rather than an adjunct of any political party. The clause was obliquely aimed at Daniel De Leon in that the abject subservience of the Socialist Trades and Labor Alliance to De Leon's Socialist Labor party provided the clearest example of what the founders did not want the IWW to become. To De Leon and representatives of the rival Socialist party of America, however, the clause represented the only expedient compromise. Both parties were cooperating in the organization of the IWW, albeit with gnashing teeth, and neither could hope to run away with the union or to tolerate its rival's seizure of it.

And therein lies the basis of factionalism within the early IWW. The factions were not based upon ideological issues. Upon the essence of the Wobbly program—that the union was an economic organization which would work toward the destruction of capitalism through direct action—all could agree. Where the nascent factions differed was upon the question of which political party, SLP or SPA, if either, would direct the IWW. The ideological diatribes prominent in the battles that followed the first convention were, in fact, smoke screens enveloping bald power struggles. Different principals at different times flitted nimbly from one "ideology" to another. If the anarchists at the convention must have scoffed at the reference to "the political field" in the Preamble which they approved, the politicalists were guilty of a more grievous reservation.

They had no intention of honoring the prohibition of political affiliation indefinitely. The organizational weakness of the original IWW was that the union was composed of groups owing allegiance first, not to the IWW, but to some individual leader or other organization.

There were several such groupings: first, the Socialist party-ites such as Algie M. Simons who visualized the IWW as an economic auxiliary to his party. Charles Moyer and several other leaders of the Western Federation of Miners looked upon the IWW as a resuscitation for the WFM's American Labor Union. In that the WFM was in 1905 a bastion of the Socialist party, Moyer and Simons found common interests. The president of the IWW, for example, Charles Sherman, faithfully represented both organizations. The next important group centered about Daniel De Leon. The STLA men remained primarily loyal to the interests of their old, now dissolved, union, and that meant to the interests of the SLP. They conceived of the IWW as the STLA with a new name and a great many more members.

Had the IWW consisted of nothing more than these groups, it would soon have been tugged into nothing. But, whatever the ulterior motives of those who agreed to the Preamble, they had given birth to an idea—of a revolutionary, economic organization free of political control—and in the process created a nucleus of the IWW which adhered to that position without mental reservation. Some of these were longstanding "unionists-first" such as William E. Trautmann. Others had been previously connected with the WFM such as Vincent St. John or the SLP such as Frank Bohn. And this group was eventually to be the undoing of the others.

The first power struggle that wracked the IWW began shortly after the founding convention had closed. That convention had elected as the union's president Charles O. Sherman of the Metal Workers. His election, as well as that of the two members of the temporary executive committee at large, was assured by the WFM, the largest component of the new organization, and was indirectly a victory for the SPA. The two members of the board at large were John Riordan of the WFM and F. W. Cronin. De Leon's group was quietly but effectively excluded. Algie Simons observed gleefully that De Leon's candidate for the board was Thomas C. Powers. De Leon seconded Powers' nomination, and De Leon's supporters made many pleas for his election. But he received only 7,189 votes to 40,446 and 33,554 for the two elected.[9] It had not taken Simons long after his convention respite to renew his attacks on the old nemesis. If the SPA were to control the new union, De Leon must be rapidly dispatched.

De Leon did not agree. In his postconvention analysis for the SLP he listed three factions "or tendencies at Chicago, each of which marked the degree to which it has emancipated itself from capitalist governmental habits of thought." These included a group which proposed state organization of industrial unions; a craft group (De Leon was here referring to Simons); and the "third group . . . that prevailed . . . that recognized the only basis upon which the administration of the Socialist Republic can be reared—industrial constituencies to the total exclusion of political constituencies." [10] By defining his factions so broadly, De Leon could include himself among the victors along with Sherman, Trautmann, Hagerty, Haywood, and Riordan. By De Leon's scorekeeping methods, the SLP had done quite well. Two of the "victorious faction," Riordan and Trautmann (the general secretary-treasurer), held offices along with Sherman.

De Leon's ideologically determined analysis was wishful

thinking. Simons more accurately portrayed the outcome of the first convention when he aligned the principals according to power groups, and the SPA group did appear to be on the verge of capturing the union. Obvious in both men's analyses is the fact that the compromise spirit of the convention was already dead. Each interpreted the event as to how well the SPA or the SLP had done compared to its rival. Soon, this spirit developed into an open split between Sherman, backed by Simons, most of the SPA men, and the WFM administration on one side, and De Leon, Trautmann, and a minor WFM organizer, Vincent St. John, on the other.

The initial issue was the WFM's opinion that, as the largest component union, it should lead the IWW. President Moyer told the 1905 WFM convention that he trusted "that realizing the absolute helplessness of organized labor as it is now constructed, that you will act fearlessly and that a message of encouragement will go out from this convention to the thousands of discouraged workers who are looking to you, confident that the Western Federation of Miners will be the vanguard of an army that will lead them to industrial liberty." [11] It is understandable that the WFM should thus conceive of itself. In addition to being the largest of the Wobbly unions, the WFM was the most dynamic union in the nation in 1905. Moyer and his ally Sherman visualized the IWW as a potentially bigger and better American Labor Union (the WFM's previous attempt to organize a national labor movement with the WFM as the "vanguard"). Simons and the SPA group were sympathetic and that was the issue.[12] Simons' preference was based on no essential ideological difference between the ALU and the STLA. He supported the former on the simple basis that the ALU was allied to the Socialist party while the STLA served a similar function for the rival Socialist Labor party.

This is the key to the split of 1906. The SPA men visualized the IWW as an economic arm for their party, and this clashed directly with De Leon's similar aspirations. The third group, allied at the time with De Leon, and led by Trautmann and St. John, insisted that the union remain independent of both parties.

De Leon, of course, was not idle. He had been accustomed to unchallenged leadership in both party and union for too long to stand aside quietly while Sherman, Moyer, and the SPA assumed control of the IWW. He did not intend to see his STLA absorbed into a rechristened ALU. Nor did De Leon have any illusions that once his old enemies were securely in control of the IWW they would continue to tolerate his presence. Thus, he girded for battle and found plenty of allies, most notably Trautmann and St. John. This group had an unexpected stroke of luck when Moyer was removed from an active role in the struggle. Early in 1906, Moyer, Haywood, and a Denver storekeeper and blacklisted miner named George Pettibone, were arrested and indicted for the murder of Frank Steunenberg, the former governor of Idaho who had been blown to pieces by an assassin's bomb when he returned to his home one evening. With both Moyer and Haywood in jail, the active direction of the WFM fell into the hands of John O'Neill who, while openly sympathetic to Sherman's cause, was of necessity more concerned with WFM than IWW matters, specifically the imminent trial of Secretary-Treasurer Haywood in Boise. Thus, De Leon, Trautmann, and St. John held an advantageous tactical position.[13]

By early 1906, privately expressed ill-feeling made it obvious that there would be a struggle for leadership at the second convention. O'Neill wrote to a moderate socialist in March that he was "sorry to learn that . . . Trautmann could find nothing more to talk about at the late protest meeting held at Indianapolis [to protest Idaho's illegal extradition of Haywood, Moyer, and Pettibone] than John Mitchell and other labor leaders." [14] It seemed to O'Neill that it was more important to attack the "anarchy of capitalism" than the AFL.

But the disdain for Trautmann's style was only a reflection of the fact that the impending split was a battle for control of the union. A few conciliators attempted to head off the split. Ernest Untermann urged the delegates to the convention not "to be misled into a *premature* endorsement of either of the present revolutionary parties in the United States." Untermann asked that the coalition character of the union be continued for the time being, with union members supporting only union activities within the union. "If the majority of you are in favor of either party," he continued, "you will support it even without a resolution, and you cannot prevent the minority from supporting whom they wish. A resolution is, therefore, useless. Let them sneer at the 'slowshulist' party [the SPA]. Let them denounce the Socialist Labor party. Let them decry all political action. Do not heed them. *The Industrial Workers of the World will find its political bearings in due time.*" [15] All was to no avail. Both factions were set on capturing the organization.

It was clear from the beginning of the convention that the Trautmann–De Leon–St. John forces claimed a majority of delegates. Sherman admitted this shortly after the convention had closed. As he described it, his faction's only hope was parliamentary: they controlled the chair and "we believed we could starve them out by obstructive tactics, but at the end of the tenth day, De Leon had a resolution passed that [the delegates] be allowed $1.50 per day as salary and expenses while attending the convention. That was more money than any of them had earned in their lives, and they were ready to stay with him until Christmas." [16]

The Trautmann–De Leon–St. John group had the day and eliminated the vestiges of Sherman's power by abolishing the office of president. The remainder of the struggle was colorful but anticlimactic. Sherman still had possession of the keys to the Chicago office of the organization (and it was an organization to which there was little more of substance than keys), and he refused to surrender them. He also retained control of the union's official organ, the *Industrial Worker*, and a small bank account. Thereupon ensued some rather unproletarian conduct on both sides. St. John, Trautmann, and several others filed for a court injunction against Sherman's retention of those IWW assets that he refused to surrender. "It would be well for the readers of the *Industrial Worker* to preserve this number," Sherman wrote, "that they may keep fresh in their memory the names of these so-called 'friends' of the working class, who seek to settle the differences existing in a labor organization through the capitalistic court." [17] The triumphant faction, on the other hand, roundly attacked Sherman on the same grounds when he hired private detectives and used the police to guard the IWW headquarters.[18] The courts and police were rather befuddled by the whole affair.

Max Hayes—the AFL Socialist who, except for Victor Berger, was the only notable socialist invited who refused to attend the original IWW convention—thoroughly enjoyed the spectacle. "That the IWW received its deathblow at Chicago and will gradually disintegrate," he wrote in November 1906, "no careful observer of labor affairs will attempt to dispute." [19] Three months later, in the same Algie Simons-edited *International Socialist Review*, Hayes mused over the IWW's: "The De Leon–Trautmann wing claims to be flapping as of yore, while

the Shermanites insist they are it with a capital 'I.' " He re-
viewed the incidents of the split and called the court's settle-
ment "a dandy straddle." According to Hayes, the court permitted the Sherman wing to keep the headquarters and the
Industrial Worker, and Trautmann could also have headquarters and as many official organs as he might need. . . .
The membership are graciously extended the extraordinary
privilege of paying dues to whomsoever they please . . . which
shows that American liberty still exists." Both sides, Hayes
concluded, claimed "a great victory." [20]

The principals of the 1906 split, like rivals in all power con-
flicts, credited the dispute with a grave ideological significance.
St. John, for the winning group, observed sometime later, that
"the administration of the IWW was in the hands of men who
were not in accord with the revolutionary program of the organization." [21] According to St. John, Sherman and his gang
were "labor fakirs" whose aims were purely reformist and parliamentarian. They were not revolutionaries at all but merely
labor leaders of the AFL type.[22] It was as if the cardinals of the
Catholic Church discovered they had elected a secret Methodist
to the papacy; when the revolutionary industrial unionists
discovered the mistake, St. John concluded, they had no choice
but to depose their rivals. The Sherman faction said that the
faction that unseated them was "an impossibilist" group following De Leon on his traditionally destructive path.[23]

These epithets were identical to those which the SLP and
the SPA had hurled at each other for six years and would continue to use for decades—slowshulist versus impossibilist. As
the dispute wore turgidly on, each faction's ideological mut-
terings became more confused and self-contradictory.

The Shermanite *Industrial Worker* wrote in early 1907
that "we, of the Industrial Workers of the World, are not to

be placed in the category of those who oppose absolutely all political action." Less than a year later, Sherman's group de-emphasized their adherence to political action. Then, according to the Sherman faction, it was "De Leon, boring from without," who "tried to use *our* Industrial Union to revive *their* skimpy political machine. For *them,* the Industrial Workers of the World was supposed to be, first, the recruiting office, and afterwards the liberal manger of the Socialist Labor party. . . *Ours* is a class politics and not a party politics." [24] The Shermanite writer maintained that his faction was the "direct actionist" group: "past experience teaches that our needs and wants can only be satisfied by that direct politics which has its starting point right where we are hived and robbed." Algie Simons, who should have been embarrassed at posing as the industrial unionist *contre* the parliamentarian, wrote after the 1906 convention that "if the IWW is wrecked on the crooked snag of De Leonism, how will those friends of industrialism who feared to say what they thought and knew at the last convention excuse themselves?" [25]

But no one was embarrassed. Both sides posed as the guardians of the industrial unionist ark as opposed to the conniving politicians of the other faction who sought only to convert the IWW into a subservient arm of their party. Both sides' analyses were half correct—in the descriptions of their opponents. Simons and Sherman and the Moyer faction of the WFM did have ulterior designs for the IWW as their opponents charged. Simons anticipated a union that would serve as a vote-getting arm of the SPA among the working class. They visualized a newer, bigger, and better ALU led by the WFM and allied to the SPA. Just the opposite held for the triumphant faction. De Leon and his STLA men visualized an organization much like Moyer's but to the benefit of their own Socialist Labor party: in short, a newer, bigger, and better STLA. Men like Trautmann and St. John, who wanted no political control, happened to fall in with De Leon solely because, at the moment, the SPA threat looked greater than the SLP's. These two were most loyal to the principles originally conceived by the IWW, that the union should be completely an economic organization, beholden to neither party and enjoying the support of both.

The Shermanites later said that the abolition of the presidency—Sherman was the first and only "president" of the IWW—was positive proof of the victors' anarchism. Although the few anarchists in the IWW did in fact support the triumphant faction, the abolition of the presidency had nothing to do with anarchism. It was an expedient tactic and nothing more. St. John later wrote that instead of untying Sherman's parliamentary knot, the "revolutionists" cut the knot by abolishing Sherman's office. It was a tactical maneuver similar to that to which it responded, what Sherman referred to cynically as his group's "obstructionism." [26] The evidence supports St. John's assertion. None of the new Wobbly leaders considered the abolition a watershed of principle, and 1906 saw no substantive change in the centralized nature of the IWW. The general secretary-treasurer simply assumed the executive powers formerly the president's.

Sherman's IWW slowly faded away, eventually selling its share of the IWW's physical facilities to the Socialist party and abandoning the field to its opponents. Most of the SPA men left the union at that time. Debs was initially unhappy with the manner in which the SPA men had acquitted themselves. He wrote during the dispute that it was likely true that De Leon had political designs upon the IWW as a means of disrupting the SPA. But, Debs continued, if De Leon succeeds, it will be because his enemies in the Socialist party, "in their bitter personal hostility to him, denounce the revolutionary IWW and support the reactionary AFL and thereby play directly into his hands." [27] Debs recognized that the split was essentially a power struggle but, once it appeared to him that De Leon was in control, he too allowed his "little red card" to lapse into inactivity. The WFM severed from the Wobblies during 1907.

The group that bested the Sherman faction in 1906 was led by Daniel De Leon, William E. Trautmann, and Vincent St. John, and was supported by the SLP men, other unionists (including many WFM men who remained with both unions), and a number of delegates to the convention who appear to have been western migrant workers. When the smoke of battle cleared, De Leon was in apparent control of the organization. The anarchists about whom Sherman made so much fuss were few in numbers and unorganized. St. John and Trautmann had joined with De Leon because they feared SPA control of the union. They did not intend, as increasingly De Leon did, to remedy SPA domination by tying the fate of the IWW to that of the SLP.

Although he called publicly for the autonomy of the union, and his theoretical writings provided a rationale for the IWW program, De Leon had thought in terms of SLP dominance from the beginning. Shortly after the first convention, he replied to a letter from a personal devotee who was disturbed at De Leon's small power under the Sherman administration. De Leon wrote:

You mention two effects as flowing from the present state of things, the first, that the abstinence of both parties from political talk at the IWW meetings has virtually come down to "no poli-

tics in the union." I think this is as it should be—FOR THE
PRESENT. At least it is unavoidable. In point of fact, seeing that
socialist economics is politics, the politics is right there. What is
absent is the concrete political party. . . . I pardon the SP's for
believing that their party will endorse the IWW. Within twelve
months they will have found out. In the meantime, we would be
playing into the hands of the AFL Kangs if we pushed the
political talk into the IWW locals, at this time.[28]

De Leon's view was to employ the IWW as a means of recruiting for the SLP. Furthermore, he felt that Wobblies formerly associated with the SPA would become disillusioned
with their party within a year when the party refused to affiliate with the IWW. Then they would turn to the obliging SLP.
Events beyond De Leon's control, however, took a different
turn, namely, the initial struggle for control between Sherman
and Trautmann. De Leon was forced to scrap his tactic of quiet
waiting. He reasoned that it was to the SLP's interests to throw
in actively against Sherman and the SPA group.

Like Sherman's conception of the IWW, De Leon's was contradictory to the avowed purpose spelled out at the original
convention. Certainly it was opposed to the views of St. John
and Trautmann before and after the 1906 split. To the IWW,
which St. John represented, the "point of fact" was not that
"socialist economics is politics" but that "socialist politics is
economics," that direct action and not the ballot box was the
route to the workers' improvement and the eventual revolution.[29]

De Leon's intentions became more obvious after the 1906
fiasco. Writing a few years later, an IWW organizer recorded
his observations of the grass-roots IWW during the period
after the 1906 split. He witnessed the founding of many "prom-
ising" locals "with much enthusiasm and goodly number." But

the enthusiasm and numbers were quickly dissipated by the efforts of SPA men and SLP men to capture the organizations for their parties, chiefly, this organizer noted, the latter. There were three elements in the locals: "raw recruits without political affiliation," SPA supporters, and advocates of affiliation with the SLP. "The two last-named elements would begin their squabbles; the raw recruits would conclude that they had come to the wrong door and would leave; followed soon by the SP's and leaving behind the SLP-ites clinging to the IWW like a drowning man to a straw." The observer concluded that "stagnation followed, and the 'local' vegetated as a mutual admiration society." De Leon had duplicated the STLA better than he wished. The doctrinal exclusiveness that had stultified the STLA worked its mischief in the IWW as well. "Further growth was rendered impossible." [30]

St. John and others among De Leon's 1906 allies were alarmed by reports of this type. They felt that they were witnessing the partisan subversion which they thought they had eliminated when they expelled Sherman. De Leon was aware of St. John's apprehension. Furthermore, De Leon was vividly aware of his own unsavory reputation among American radicals. Within a few months after the Sherman group's final capitulation, De Leon was searching for a front man to confound his possible rivals but he approached the wrong one.

Recalling that Big Bill Haywood had reacted equivocally to the 1906 split when Moyer and most of the WFM leadership stood loyally by Sherman, and quite aware of Haywood's great prestige among radicals after the Boise trial, De Leon wrote to the miner, feeling him out, in August 1907. He hinted at a possible second split which was due to the fact that "however undeserved they were, those who have been early in the struggle have necessarily drawn upon themselves animosities." What was "worse yet," those animosities tended to disqualify "such organizations and their spokesmen for the work of themselves speedily effecting unification." But, fortuitously, "the capitalist class, through this late persecution of you, has 'produced' the unifier." [31]

Haywood may well have been flattered by De Leon's attentions and the implication that he was indispensable to the IWW. But during the summer of 1907 Haywood was the object of a great deal of attention and was, in fact, about to set out on a whirlwind lecture tour for the SPA when he received De Leon's letter.

Moreover, Haywood was a member of the Socialist party and, after Boise, a rather celebrated member. He shared the suspicion in which most of the SPA held the "ubiquitous Dan." Finally, Haywood had never *approved* De Leon's part in the 1906 dispute; he had merely taken a position less partisan than Moyer's. He chose a similar neutralist position in 1907 and 1908.

A more significant aspect of De Leon's letter made it quite clear that he understand the IWW as an adjunct of the SLP. Haywood no doubt understood, De Leon continued, "as the Socialist Labor Party does, that, without the industrially economic organization of the workers, the day of the workers' victory at the polls . . . would be the day of their defeat." Lest Haywood misunderstand his rhetorical slap at SPA political action, De Leon added that "the day . . . when the IWW will have reflected its own political party [the SLP], in other words, the day when the vicious nonsense of 'pure and simple political socialism' will be at an end, it will be with a shout of joy that the SLP will break ranks." [32] That the SLP would benefit in the meantime by IWW organization was clear enough. Haywood was not attracted by De Leon's offer. He had been imprisoned almost since the founding of the IWW and was, in 1907, more interested in his work with the Socialist party than with the IWW. De Leon did not win him over.

As expected, the split came at the fourth IWW convention, held in 1908. The issue through which De Leon was dumped from his incomplete dominance of the IWW was the revision of the Wobbly Preamble, specifically, the second paragraph. The revision was the tactic for toppling De Leon just as the abolition of the presidency in 1906 had been a tactic in eliminating Sherman. The disputed phrase was that between the oppressors and the oppressed "a struggle must go on until all the toilers come together on the political as well as on the industrial field." [33] St. John, who now had the same coalition behind him as that in which De Leon had shared in 1906, packed the convention with an "overalls brigade." These delegates were largely migrant workers, unemployed at the time, who had come to the Chicago meeting on the rails and on foot. Their numbers gave St. John voting control of the convention and he deleted the so-called "political clause" in favor of a new paragraph which omitted all mention of political action:

> Between these two classes a struggle must go on until the workers of the world organize as a class, take possession of the earth and the machinery of production, and abolish the wage system.[34]

De Leon reacted by dubbing the delegates "the bummery," a name which they accepted with an ironic shrug and a song, "Hallelujah, I'm a Bum!" De Leon claimed that the organization had been captured by antipolitical anarchists (of whom St. John was the "arch-fakir") who had completely destroyed the original intention of the union.[35] In that many of the "bummery" came from Washington State where anarchist ideas were in vogue among radicals, there probably were some anarchists in the group. But De Leon's accusation that the union had become "an anarchistic wild offshoot of the bona fide IWW" was invalid.

The deletion of the "political clause" was a tactic. It was not intended to place and did not place the IWW in an inflexible antipolitical actionist position. Rather, it was intended to force De Leon into a tacit admission of his plans for the IWW. St. John's position was not antipolitical but nonpolitical in the sense that even the deleted Preamble was nonpolitical. His supporters sought a union "without affiliation with any political party." It had become increasingly obvious to them that De Leon did not share their view, and they settled upon a change in wording in the original Preamble as a means of purging De Leon.

Frank Bohn, who came into the IWW with De Leon's STLA but remained with the IWW in 1908, summed up his position shortly before the convention showdown. One consideration alone, he said, had given him cause for sustaining the SLP since the founding of the IWW. That was his hope that the IWW men in the SLP would become at least equal with non-IWW members. The opposite had occurred. De Leon obviously planned to subordinate union to party and not vice versa. As Bohn noted, "the current events are showing what a drag upon the IWW the SLP is proving itself to be." [36]

The many Wobbly protestations of political interest after 1908 indicate that the union did not become either anarchist or syndicalist. Officially, the union remained as it had always officially been, a nonpolitical working-class organization. St. John was no anarchist or syndicalist. Elizabeth Gurley Flynn remembered him after his death as "one of the clearest thinkers in the IWW [who] fought consistently to save it from becoming a tail to the kites of Daniel De Leon and the Socialist Labor Party on the one hand and what he contemptuously called 'the Anarchist freaks' on the other." She added, "He tried hard to make it a militant industrial union." [37]

Later Wobblies were sensitive to De Leon's accusations and went to great pains to answer them. *Solidarity,* the organ of the eastern wing of the IWW, wrote that the fourth convention "applied the knife to the ulcer of political secretarianism" and not to political action itself. In fact, the IWW did not intend "to allow the equally fatal ulcer of anti-political sectarianism to develop in its place. And if it does, in our opinion the knife will have to be applied again, and the sooner the better." [38] Some months later, the same journal continued its analysis of the split: "The IWW at its birth was committed to a program of 'political action' while at the same time forbidden to endorse or affiliate with any 'political party.' Thus, the 'political' sectarians were afforded a common vantage ground whereupon they might meet and attack each other, using the IWW as a scapegoat for their mutual tribulations. And the IWW must not attempt to come back at them. No individual member, even, must be allowed to attack either 'political party,' because that would be attacking 'political action,' you know, which was 'treason' to the Preamble." [39] It was for this reason that the Preamble was altered.

By 1911, even the anarchist Wobblies from Washington State admitted, albeit regretfully, that the clause was altered not as a repudiation of all political action but because the clause had been a cover for the two Socialist parties' attempts to capture the union. "The clause was stricken from the Preamble," wrote *The Agitator* (which had left the IWW in favor of William Z. Foster's Syndicalist League of North America) "because of its misinterpretation by the ballot box element."

Elizabeth Flynn said that the split "was a revolt against De Leon's attempt to tie the industrial union movement to the apron strings of the Socialist Labor party." [40] Justus Ebert, a Wobbly scholar-polemicist, interpreted the original IWW as an attempt to unite the leading Socialist economic and political tendencies of the country. The attempt failed; Ebert said, "The two Socialist parties made the IWW a battleground for their own supremacy. The IWW, as a matter of self-preservation, had to get rid, first of one, then of the other." [41]

St. John was in essential agreement. According to Covington Hall, who was the leader of the Louisiana Wobblies, one of the few viable local organizations, St. John had been hesitant about leading the revolt against De Leon. Hall told St. John in 1908 that "unless we take the politicalists by the nape of the neck and seat of the britches and throw them out of the doors and windows, the IWW is lost." St. John agreed, adding after the fact was accomplished, "I do not know if the organization can stand the strain, but it was the only thing left us to do if we were to save it." [42]

Covington Hall was skeptical about all political action but it was St. John, and not he, who emerged from the 1908 convention as the power in the IWW. St. John noted later that his objection to De Leon was that De Leon and the SLP "were trying to bend the IWW to their purpose." The struggle was one for control between industrial unionists and the SLP partisans because the former had no intention of allowing the latter "to control the organization." [43] William Bohn, a confidant of many Wobbly leaders, also denied that the struggle was over the usefulness of political action as a principle. The SLP was "attempting to make the union subordinate to the political party." The SLP men were purged not because the IWW "did not believe in the uses of political activity, but because it was deemed desirable to escape entirely from the influence of politics and politicians." [44]

In conclusion, the split of 1908 was based on an issue scarcely more ideological than the split of two years before. It was a power struggle between two groups, one of which sought to subordinate the IWW to the SLP, while the other sought a union independent of all political party control. Both sides publicly espoused the same ideology. De Leon's later assertion that he had been thrown out by anarchists was a groundless canard.[45] It was the same accusation that Sherman had made of the De Leon–Trautmann–St. John group in 1906. The alliance that unseated De Leon was the same group with which he had been allied in 1906. The official IWW position on political action (including De Leon's public pronouncements in 1905, Sherman's in 1906, St. John's in 1908, and Haywood's in 1912) remained essentially unchanged: no politics in the union. It can be questioned, of course, whether or not De Leon or any of the others were completely candid in their statements but this is of secondary relevance; the *IWW*'s avowed position did not change after either 1906 or 1908.

Overwhelmed at the 1908 convention, the De Leonites bolted the IWW, maintaining weakly that they had "expelled the anarchists." On that premise, they established their own IWW with headquarters in Detroit from which the union received its usual name—the Detroit IWW as opposed to St. John's Chicago IWW. The Detroit Wobblies retained the original Preamble, published a few newspapers, and organized several locals but for the most part had little success. Most of their publications were concerned with attacking the Chicago "anarchists."

De Leon had returned to diatribes against rival radicals, a familiar ground. After an interlude of three years, he had another STLA: tiny and sectarian but, at least, securely under his and the SLP's control. The Detroit IWW had a local in Paterson, New Jersey, when the textile strike of 1913 broke out (as the Chicago IWW did not) but it was the St. John–Haywood IWW that took over the direction of the strike. De Leon's group continued downhill. In 1914 the masquerade was obviously over. The Detroit group renamed itself the Workers International Industrial Union. The membership of the WIIU never exceeded ten thousand and, with no known mourners, it was dissolved in 1925.[46]

NOTES

1. Quoted in Elizabeth Gurley Flynn, *I Speak My Own Piece: Autobiography of the Rebel Girl* (New York: International Publishing Co., 1955), p. 161.

2. *Proceedings of the First Convention of the IWW* (New York: 1905), pp. 85–86; *ISR*, vol. 6 (August, 1905).

3. *Proceedings of the First Convention*, p. 28.

4. *Proceedings of the First Convention*, p. 28.

5. Robert F. Hoxie, *Trade Unionism in the United States*, 2d. ed. (New York: D. Appleton and Co., 1923), p. 142.

6. Max Hayes, "World of Labor," *ISR* 7 (February, 1907): 502.

7. See Abbe Hacker, "The Anarchist Influence on the IWW 1905–1913: An Outline," typescript, Vertical File, Labadie Collection, University of Michigan; Paul F. Brissenden, *The Launching of the Industrial Workers of the World* (Berkeley: University of California Press, 1913), p. 40.

8. The original Preamble may be found in the *Proceedings of the First Convention* or in virtually every other Wobbly publication before 1908 (when it was revised). A more convenient source is Joyce Kornbluh, *Rebel Voices: An I.W.W. Anthology* (Ann Arbor: University of Michigan Press, 1965), p. 12.

9. Algie M. Simons, "Industrial Workers of the World," *ISR* 6 (August, 1905): 76.

10. *Daily People*, September 6, 1905.

11. *Western Federation of Miners: Proceedings of the Thirteenth An-*

nual Convention, 1905 (Denver: Western Federation of Miners, 1905), p. 21.

12. See the editorial, *ISR* 6 (March, 1905): 564.

13. For a discussion of the Haywood affair, see Joseph R. Conlin, "The Haywood Case: An Enduring Riddle," *Pacific Northwest Quarterly,* January, 1968, pp. 23–32 and *Big Bill Haywood and the Radical Union Movement* (Syracuse: 1969).

14. John M. O'Neill to Adolf Germer, March 24, 1906, Germer Papers, State Historical Society of Wisconsin; see also Algie M. Simons to May Wood Simons, April 3, 1906, Simons Papers, State Historical Society of Wisconsin. Simons names Trautmann as the instigator of the revolt.

15. *Industrial Worker,* June, 1906. Emphasis mine.

16. *Record Herald* (Chicago), October 7, 1906.

17. *Industrial Worker,* January, 1907.

18. "To Whom It May Concern," IWW leaflet (January 5, 1907), IWW Collection, State Historical Society of Wisconsin.

19. Max Hayes, "World of Labor," *ISR* 7 (November, 1906): 312.

20. Hayes, "World of Labor," *ISR* 7 (February, 1907): 502.

21. Vincent St. John, *The IWW: Its History, Methods, and Structure* (Chicago: IWW Publishing Bureau, 1916), p. 6.

22. Quoted in John Graham Brooks, *American Syndicalism: The IWW* (New York: Macmillan Co., 1913), p. 85.

23. Charles O. Sherman to Morris Hillquit, February 2, 1907, Hillquit Papers, State Historical Society of Wisconsin.

24. *Industrial Worker,* January, 1907. Emphasis mine.

25. Editorial, *ISR* 7 (October, 1906): 243.

26. St. John, *The IWW* (Chicago: IWW Publishing Bureau, 1917), p. 6.

27. *The Worker* (New York), August, 1906; *Daily People,* August 12, 1906.

28. Daniel De Leon to Olive M. Johnson, November 29, 1905, quoted in *Daniel De Leon: The Man and His Work, A Symposium* (New York: Socialist Labor Party Press, 1920), pp. 104–105. Capitals in original.

29. St. John, *The IWW* (Chicago: IWW Publishing Bureau, 1916), p. 41.

30. *Solidarity,* March 25, 1911. The observer was either B. H. Williams or C. H. McCarthy.

31. Daniel De Leon to William D. Haywood, August 3, 1907, *De Leon Symposium,* p. 59.

32. De Leon to Haywood, August 3, 1907, *De Leon Symposium,* p. 60.

33. See virtually any pre-1908 Wobbly publication or Kornbluh, *Rebel Voices,* p. 12.

34. See Kornbluh, *Rebel Voices,* p. 13.

35. "The Industrial Workers of the World," IWW pamphlet (1908?), IWW Collection, State Historical Society of Wisconsin.

36. "The Failure to Attain Socialist Unity," *ISR* 8 (June, 1908): 755.

37. Flynn, *I Speak My Own Piece,* p. 192.

38. *Solidarity*, July 23, 1910.

39. *Solidarity*, March 26, 1911.

40. *The Agitator*, August 1, 1911; Flynn, *I Speak My Own Piece*, pp. 84, 192.

41. Justus Ebert, *L'IWW Nella Teoria E Nella Pràtica* [The IWW in theory and practice] 5th rev. ed. (n.p., 1937), pp. 54–55.

42. Covington Hall, "Labor Struggles in the Deep South," typescript, Labor History Archives, Wayne State University, p. 230.

43. St. John, *The IWW* (Chicago: IWW Publishing Bureau, 1919), pp. 9, 19.

44. "Industrial Workers of the World," *The Survey* 28 (May 4, 1912): 222. For a more recent analysis along the same lines, see Fred Thompson, *The IWW: Its First Fifty Years* (Chicago: IWW Publishing Bureau, 1955), p. 40.

45. *Daily People*, April 2, 13, 1913.

46. Walter Galenson, *Rival Unionism in the United States* (New York: Russell & Russell, 1940), p. 8; Leon Wolman, *Ebb and Flow in Trade Unionism* (New York: National Bureau of Economic Research, 1936), pp. 190–191.

3

Whipping Boys, Practical Men, and Other Undesirables

IF the worst historical distortion of the IWW was that it was "syndicalist," the spirits of the Wobblies would have petty cause for complaint. But the scholars have not let the Wobblies off quite so easily. Historians have approached the subject from three directions. A first, small group has been content to repeat the intemperate denunciations of the IWW's many contemporary enemies. They have seen the Wobblies as dangerous, destructive villains, much as did the *San Diego Tribune* when members of the union were numerous in Southern California. Hanging was too good for Wobblies, the *Tribune* felt, and

they would be much better dead, for they are absolutely useless in the human economy; they are the waste material of creation and should be drained off into the sewer of oblivion there to rot in cold obstruction like any other excrement.[1]

The Wobblies were obligingly defunct by the time most historical accounts were written so the historians have generally transcended the *Tribune*'s spleen. But the San Diego editor's assumptions endure. As late as 1968, a historian of the American Southwest nonchalantly shrugged away the atrocious deportation from Bisbee, Arizona, into the New Mexico desert of some 1,200 Wobblies "and other undesirables." [2]

Most historians have been more sympathetic. A second approach to the subject has commiserated with the working-class desperation to which the IWW responded. These historians have scolded the Wobblies only for their alleged methods: violence, sabotage, terror. Even these were understandable, the sympathetic historians note: the exploitation of the western migrant workers was so extreme that the members of the IWW had been completely alienated from American social values.

A third vision of the Wobblies has focused on their irrepressible spirit. Wallace Stegner felt that "no thoroughly adequate history of the IWW exists" because the historical accounts of the movement "lack the kind of poetic understanding which should invest any history of a militant church." [3] Indeed, the IWW enhanced their most mundane activities with a salty imagination and zest. In the East, an IWW tactic for winning public sympathy during a strike involved dispatching en masse the strikers' ragged children to "safer" homes in other cities. The exodus relaxed the strain on strike funds and, accompanied by a great deal of ballyhoo, effectively portrayed employers as starvers of children. In 1913, the IWW produced a "pageant" at Madison Square Garden that dramatized the silk weavers' strike then underway in Paterson, New Jersey. Designed to raise money, the Pageant was cast by the workers themselves. While a financial failure, it was accounted a theatrical sensation. In the Pacific Northwest, Wobblies organized brass bands parodying the Salvation Army's famous ensembles and sang sarcastic revolutionary lyrics to old gospel hymns. A few of their numbers, like Joe Hill's *Pie in the Sky,* survive in folksong repertories today.

Despite their diversity, all three historical approaches have one point in common. Hostile, patronizing, or romantic, the historians have implicitly agreed that the IWW was an aberration. They see the union either as dangerously antipathetic to American traditions or as ineffective because of the Wobblies' extreme alienation from the greater society or as just a colorful ragtag bunch of poetic visionaries in a hard-nosed practical country.

The arguments of each school have their germs of validity but it seems a more profitable approach to the study of the IWW to understand that the Wobblies were in reality more like than unlike their conventional contemporaries. The Wobblies were, after all, molded and formed by the same forces that acted in some degree upon the whole of American society. A look at them with some emphasis on the values they held in common with early twentieth-century Americans rather than on their peculiarities will reveal that the IWW moved with the American mainstream at least as regularly as it bucked the current.

The IWW has been classed as an aberrant movement because it is charged: the union sanctioned violence and sabotage; scorned political action and violated the nation's commitment to democratic political process. Finally, the IWW has been characterized as un-American, an alien ideological import into a pragmatic country. The final point requires the least comment. With the exception of a few Italian leaders during the union's brief era in the industrial East, the IWW was headed throughout its history by natives bred in an emphatically American milieu. The most famous of them, William D. "Big Bill" Haywood, might have sneered that his family was "so American that if traced back it would probably run to the Puritan bigots or the cavalier pirates" but he saw fit to note his ancestry anyway. Other Wobbly leaders sported similar genealogies and constantly looked to American precedents such as the Revolution, John Brown, Abraham Lincoln, and even historian Frederick Jackson Turner for their historical corroboration rather than to a European revolutionary tradition. Few Wobbly membership lists survive but police records of mass arrests of Wobblies on the West Coast during the early 1910s show a ratio between native and foreign-born pretty much like the cross-section of the region's population.[4]

The Wobblies' reputation for violence is scarcely more valid. It is fruitless and immediately beside the point to argue whether or not American society is inherently violent or more violent than others. The point is that the IWW's reputation for riot and incendiarism is quite fallacious. Former Wobbly Ralph Chaplin was correct when he blamed the historians' vision of the IWW "as a conspiracy of alien arsonists and dynamiters" on their "using the hysterical newspaper headlines of the day as source material."[5] As Richard Brazier, another old Wobbly, wrote, "the IWW, of course, never did have a 'good press' and we were more or less accustomed to being made the whipping boys for something we knew nothing about."[6] A contemporary student of the IWW, sociologist Carlton Parker, observed that "some important portion of IWW terrors can be traced directly to the inarticulated public demand that the IWW news story produce a thrill."[7] But whatever the source of the image, it was and remains a canard. Far from advocating violence, the IWW felt that violence was unnecessary and destructive of its cause. The Wobblies re-

peatedly urged prudence upon impulsive members and, on
numerous occasions, acted positively to avert incidents. When,
for example, in January 1909, a crowd of several thousand
men threatened to attack an employment agency in Spokane,
Washington, a Wobbly leader arrived just in time to cool the
crowd and invite it to a discussion meeting at the Wobbly Hall.
There he persuaded them that agents provocateurs in their
midst were egging them on in an effort to provide an excuse for
police intervention.[8]

In political America, the Wobblies are often adjudged irrelevant because of their disinterest in exerting power and effecting changes through democratic and parliamentary political
procedures. In truth, the IWW was organizationally uninterested in political action, and the western Wobblies particularly so. But this state of affairs derived less from any alienation from American traditions than from the simple reality
that most western Wobblies could not vote. They were migrant
workers, the nature of whose lives made them "homeless men"
and placed them outside the political system. They could not
meet the most liberal residency requirements. Thus, there was
no question of abrogating the anti-IWW ordinances in Spokane, San Diego, and a dozen other western cities through
the ballot. The men affected were workers who followed the
harvests and the construction camps during the summer and
settled in the cities only during their idle seasons. Like most
policies deriving from specific conditions, Wobbly nonpoliti-
calism broke down when conditions varied. Wobblies and
members of the strictly political Socialist party in the Northwest sometimes used the same persons as their delegates; apparently, the membership must have overlapped.[9]

But the question of the IWW's commonality with early
twentieth-century American society ultimately rests not upon

the illegitimacy of the union's historical image but upon the nature of the union's positive acts. The IWW's Free Speech Fights have generally been the property of the romanticizers. Between 1909, when the Wobblies first employed the tactic in Missoula, Montana, and 1916, when they abandoned the policy, the IWW staged its battles in twenty-six cities, principally in Washington, Oregon, and California.[10] The pattern of the fights varied little from city to city. The usual precipitant was a Wobbly street-speaking campaign focused on a specific issue, often the corrupt practices of employment agencies which the casual laborers frequented. City councils responded to agency pressures with ordinances prohibiting soapbox speaking. The Los Angeles ordinance was typical:

> It shall be unlawful for any person to discuss, expound, advocate or oppose the principles or creed of any political party, partisan body, or organization, or religious denomination or sect, or *the doctrines* of any *economic* or social system in any public speech, lecture, or discourse, made or delivered in any public park in the City of Los Angeles.[11]

The ordinances were clearly aimed at the IWW; Spokane's law exempted the Salvation Army, the only other organization much involved in street speaking. San Diego's ban was restricted to the tenderloin district where the casual laborers congregated.[12] And when President Taft visited Spokane during the dispute over the ordinance and spoke on the streets, a Wobbly commented sardonically:

> The law. The law must be upheld. Taft can speak on the street, and pack it for blocks—yes, so tight that workmen could not get home to their dinner. He was not put in the sweat box. He was not even arrested, although the ordinance was in effect at the time. . . . Taft held up a bundle of papers and said, "This was

handed me by the Chamber of Commerce, and you will have to
stand for it." As it was impossible to move for two hours, we
stood for it. The *Spokesman-Review* says the people don't want
to have the revolutionary harangues of the IWW speakers rammed
down their throats. Hundreds of people did not want the harangue
of the Chamber of Commerce rammed down their throats by Taft,
but they had to stand for it.[13]

But the IWW did not "stand for it." They deliberately defied
the law with the object of packing the jails beyond the city's
resources to maintain them and clogging the judicial process
through demanding individual trials, thus shifting the burden
of enforcement from the violator to the enforcer. It was civil
disobedience of the sort made famous by the civil rights dem-
onstrators of the early 1960s.

In Missoula, where authorities were flabbergasted by the
cheerful lawbreakers, the Wobblies won an easy victory. In
Spokane and other cities, things were more difficult. Authorities attempted to meet mass violation with mass arrests (103
soapboxers were arrested on the first day of the Spokane fight,
500 within a month) and by torture within the city jails. Policemen beat the jailed Wobblies in Missoula. In Spokane, thirty-
six prisoners were forced into a Black Hole of Calcutta so
small that several policemen were required to close the door.
Other Wobblies were moved alternately from a freezing to a
steaming hot cell. In San Diego, a mob kidnapped a Wobbly
sympathizer and mutilated him with lighted cigars. In Fresno,
men were beaten and hosed and forced to stand knee-deep in
water throughout a night.[14]

Whether or not the IWW won its fights usually depended
upon how much adverse publicity the town in question was
willing to bear. Spokane's city council capitulated after the
national press publicized the city's "barbarism" with lines

such as a reporter's plaint that "if men had murdered my own mother, I could not see them tortured as I saw IWW men tortured in the city jail." [15] San Diego's city fathers were sterner and they put the Wobblies to rout.

The Free Speech Fights were certainly thrilling events, full of the color, drama, and little ironies of which the Wobblies and their chroniclers were fond. In order to pack the jails it was necessary to place on the soapbox many Wobblies who were not polished speakers. In Spokane, one such Wobbly mounted the platform and began with the usual salutation, "Friends and Fellow Workers." This had been the signal for the police to move in and arrest the violator. But there was no policeman available, unfortunately for the unprepared Wobbly who, with a bad case of stage jitters, shouted "Where are the cops?" to the hilarity of his audience.[16] The IWW solved this problem by assigning nonorators to read from the Constitution or Declaration of Independence. In terms of propaganda, the practice carried with it the fringe benefit of men under arrest for reciting the basic law of the land. But nothing better illustrates the spirit in which the Wobblies carried out their serious business than a letter received in Spokane at the height of the battle:

> Ione, Ore., Jan. 7th, 1910
>
> Fellow Worker:
>
> A Demonstration was just held in Sheep Camp No. 1 there being three present, a herder and two dogs. The following resolutions were adopted:
>
> Resolved, That we send $10.00 for the free speech fight in Spokane.
>
> Yours for liberty,
> THOS. J. ANDERSON
>
> P.S.—Stay with it. I'm coming.—T.J.A.[17]

The color surrounding the disputes is too vivid to ignore. But what, in essence, were the Free Speech Fights all about? They were certainly not revolutionary. They were joined to preserve—locally to reassert—a right with a Constitutional Article and a century of tradition behind it. The IWW's interest in street speaking was not even based primarily on a desire to preach revolution; they wanted the streets open for the purpose of organizing a union. "These fights were deemed necessary to organization," a Wobbly theorist wrote. "It was thought that without street meetings, . . . the jobless, homeless migratory workers could not be organized." [18] The free speechers in Missoula and Spokane sought to hold forth on a topic no more incendiary than the corruptions of the "job sharks," agencies which commonly defrauded the casual laborers. In San Diego the Wobblies fought their battle in league with American Federation of Labor men, moderate socialists, single-taxers, and liberals, none of whom were likely to condone anarchistic jeremiads. Hardly confrontations between wild-eyed nihilists and men of the golden mean, the IWW's free speech fights could more accurately be described as disputes between defenders of traditional rights and corrupt interests willing to trample on the same. To label the Wobblies as nothing more than Jeffersonian libertarians would be ludicrous, but neither were their battles hostile or irrelevant to American values. Indeed, when the IWW's General Executive Board finally abandoned the Free Speech Fights in 1916, it was partly due to a pang of revolutionary conscience. Their explanation was that a revolutionary union had more germane tasks at hand than the defense of bourgeois liberties against the bourgeoisie.

It also bears mention that the allegedly lawless IWW pursued its objectives within the spirit of the law. That is, although the union systematically violated the restrictive ordinances, it did so not with criminal intent but in order to test and repeal them, in much the same spirit as John Scopes defied the Tennessee antievolution law and the Schechter brothers the National Recovery Act. The IWW was not interested in lawbreaking as such but in demonstrating the injustice of the law through the witness of their imprisonment and the infeasibility of the law through the disruption caused by its enforcement. If this is not the most desirable means of political expression in a stable society, neither is it antisocial. In view of the Wobblies' political impotence, it was their only alternative.

The IWW affected a great deal of scorn for the law in its propaganda. Bill Haywood told a federal investigating commission that he had been plastered up with injunctions so often that he did not need a pair of pants. But, in practice, the IWW evinced a regard for keeping within the law which, if grudging, was also circumspect. A Washington State woman testified that she had heard speeches by every major Wobbly agitator in the region and had never heard one "advocate or teach crime." And injunction-beclothed Bill Haywood did not shy away from using the courts, injunctions, and esoteric writs of certiorari when he could benefit from them. Haywood's implicit faith in American jurisprudence, in fact, was greater than reality warranted. He insisted that Wobblies indicted for sedition during the World War surrender and stand trial rather than go underground. "Ten thousand crimes!" Haywood snorted. "If they can make the American people or any fair-minded jury believe that, I don't see how they'll do it." Even after conviction, Haywood and Ralph Chaplin remained convinced that the Supreme Court would reverse the decision.[19] John Reed put it succinctly:

They still believe in constitutions, and the phrases of governments
—yes, in spite of the preamble, the IWW still have faith in the
goodness of mankind, and the possibility of justice for the
righteous.[20]

In view of the cynicism with which the Wobblies were prosecuted in so many of their cases, the IWW had a more promis-
ing vision of the law than its enforcers.

Finally, quite out of keeping with the reputation for re-
calcitrance foisted upon the Wobblies by their enemies and
their historians, the IWW proved willing and often adept at
negotiation and compromise. The Spokane tangle was settled
on such terms. The city agreed to abrogate the obnoxious
ordinance, to release all Wobblies held in violation of it, and
to cease harassing the IWW's newspaper, *The Industrial
Worker*. For their part, the Wobblies agreed to discontinue
street speaking and demonstration until the ordinance could
be officially repealed and to withdraw several suits they had
filed charging corruption against city officials. In San Diego
the IWW agreed to a compromise solution worked out by a
citizen's group which proscribed but did not prohibit public
speeches. The plan provided that the IWW would inform
the police three days in advance of all street meetings. The
city council rejected the plan, preferring to fight the battle
to its bitter end. Despite their numerical strength in the area,
Wobblies in Aberdeen, Washington, offered to end a dispute
during the fall of 1911 on the basis of the status quo ante but,
again, the city council elected to prosecute its war on the
organization.[21]

The image of the Wobblies as contemptuous of conventional society ignores the IWW's frequent solicitude of public
favor. The union was vividly aware of the value of a favorable

public opinion. An outraged citizenry had played a crucial role in the Wobbly victories in Spokane in 1909 and in a textile workers' strike in Lawrence, Massachusetts, in 1912. More often, as the union was also aware, a newspaper-molded public opinion was hostile to its purposes.

To judge the Wobblies by their hopeless newspaper image is to lose sight of the union's many supporters among "respectable" and moderate elements in the population. Herman Tucker, an employee of the United States Forestry Department in Missoula, was an example. During the free speech fight there in 1909, Tucker was watching from the window of his second-story office when a young logger was arrested on the corner below for reading from the Declaration of Independence. Although not especially sympathetic to the Wobblies, Tucker was incensed by the mockery of the arrest, rushed downstairs, mounted the vacant platform, and continued the reading. He, too, was arrested.[22]

On November 5, 1916, a group of Wobblies boarded the passenger boat, *Verona,* bound from Seattle for Everett, Washington, a lumber-mill town from which the IWW had been forcibly expelled a short time before. When the *Verona* docked, it was confronted by an armed posse under Sheriff Donald McRae of Snohomish County, and a gunfight erupted. The *Verona* escaped into Puget Sound by snapping its shore lines, and passengers counted between five and eleven dead and thirty-one wounded. Many of Everett's citizens angrily blamed the incident on Sheriff McRae. Some openly expressed the hope that the IWW would return and clear the town of its legal terrorists, and some merchants felt constrained to announce that they were not members of the Commercial Club which backed McRae. Mayor Gill of Seattle issued an angry public attack on McRae, denouncing the sheriff's pretentious deportation of the Wobblies and accusing him of full responsibility for the massacre. Gill dramatized his partisanship by sending gifts to the Wobblies in jail.[23]

Elmer Smith, a young lawyer in Centralia, Washington, became legal advisor to the IWW Local in that city shortly before Armistice Day, 1919, when parading American Legionnaires attacked the IWW hall and, before the day was done, lynched a Wobbly still in his army uniform, Wesley Everest. Several members of the Legion were killed during the fracas, and Elmer Smith was indicted as accessory to the crime along with ten men who had actually been present during the battle. Smith and one other defendant were acquitted. Smith subsequently devoted more than a year to organizing meetings throughout the Pacific Northwest on behalf of those still imprisoned. In 1922, he moved to California where he continued to attack the laws and trials which made convicts of men he regarded as innocent victims.[24]

The list could go on but would demonstrate only that many conventional middle-class Americans perceived the Wobblies in terms other than those of the union's usual unsavory image. The cases of Tucker, Gill, and Smith were not so isolated as to be negligible and indicate that the IWW commanded more widespread support than nihilists could reasonably expect. Men like Tucker, Gill, and Smith would not be likely to collaborate with or defend an organization of cutthroats. They knew that the IWW was not quite what its enemies depicted.

And, of course, it was not. Far from being "a conspiracy of alien arsonists and dynamiters, the purpose of which was to place all law-abiding citizens at the mercy of the mob," the IWW was in many western towns composed of just ordinary "law-abiding citizens" whose only aberration was a wretched standard of living which they attributed to the greed of capital.

Another forgotten facet of the IWW was that it served in many of the mining, smelter, railroad, and lumber-mill towns of the West as a social organization, a workingman's fraternal lodge. The IWW hall was most of the time not used for planning strikes but as a library and reading room, casual rendezvous, and dance hall. In a sense, the IWW was a surrogate church, a focal point for the social life of the laborers in the dismal and isolated industrial towns of the region. That is not a very colorful picture, calculated to appeal to romanticizers, but it is a facet of the IWW depicted in a dozen old photographs, and it places the union somewhat this side of un-American activities.

The IWW did not consider itself alien or irrelevant to accepted mores and assumed it deserved support from non-proletarians. "The IWW does not give me the right to act against the common good," the *Industrial Union Bulletin* stated as early as 1907. "There is no such thing as the right to do as I please." [25] Wobbly theorist, Justus Ebert felt that progressives and liberals should support the IWW because to them "the IWW is the proletarian forerunner of the new society, the militant protestant against capitalist reaction." [26] The claim was less a statement of fact than a plea, for Ebert added appreciatively that progressive support was frequently responsible for Wobbly successes. The Wobblies continued to appeal to the middle class. During a trial of Wobblies in Marysville, California, in 1913 for incidents arising from a riot on a hop ranch near Wheatland, the IWW solicited assistance from, among other groups, the "Women's Clubs of California." As you are women, the letter read, "we are sure of your sympathy for the men now facing death and for their innocent families." [27] It was hardly the Manifesto of the cartoon-caricatured anarchist.

Nor was the statement of William D. Haywood that if the
Wobblies involved in the Centralia Massacre were guilty,
they should be punished.[28] Haywood, in fact, the undisputed
leader of the union by the time of World War I, effected
numerous accommodations which he hoped would gain the
union public acceptance, if not public favor. He urged members of the union not to emphasize their opposition to the
war and conscription but to concentrate on trade union goals.
He understood the havoc that patriotic passions could wreak
on the union and hoped to avoid them. During the war,
Haywood saw that potentially offensive lyrics in the IWW's
"Little Red Songbook" were deleted. After the war, Haywood's
assistant and confidant, Ralph Chaplin, tried to steer the
IWW in a technocratic direction, to transform the union into
something of a research bureau, which would collect and publish information on the American economy because a "high
class educational program would add to the prestige of the
IWW while it was under attack from so many quarters." [29]

One of the most curious and obscure Wobbly activities
during the era was the organization's tacit support of Prohibition. The idea of roughhewn Wobblies pulling alongside blue-
stockinged Republican dowagers and clerical conservatives in
what was the safest conventional piety of the day seems preposterous if one persists in envisioning the Wobblies as nothing
more than erratic Reds. But the Wobblies' reasons for supporting Prohibition did not in fact differ radically from the
arguments of the middle-class drys. According to C. H. Lam-
bert, a leading California Wobbly, in 1916, Prohibition would
"make labor more efficient" and provide more work for members of the union. He predicted victory for two Prohibition
amendments then up for referendum in the state with the
implication that Wobblies would support them at the polls.[30]

The Wobblies also regarded the saloon as the stalking ground for detectives and thugs hired to provoke strikers into brawls. During a strike against contractors laying track for the Canadian Pacific Railroad in 1913, the union ordered a boycott of the saloons. The Chief of Police of Grand Junction, Colorado, observed that the Wobblies of his acquaintance "will not permit a member to drink and travel with them." [31] And the organization eventually adopted a bylaw that provided:

> Any officer or employee of any part of the Industrial Workers of the World seen in public in a state of intoxication shall, upon sufficient proof, be at once removed from his position by the proper authorities having jurisdiction over such an officer or employee, and upon conviction, shall not be eligible to hold office in any part of the organization for two years thereafter.[32]

One wonders if the American Legion had any regulations so prim.

After Prohibition became a fact, the "lawless" IWW sometimes contributed its services to enforcing the law. During a strike in the Gray's Harbor District of Washington in 1923, a Wobbly Local informed "all bootleggers and gambling houses" that "you are hereby given notice to close up during the strike or drastic action will be taken against you." Wobblies in Portland, Spokane, and Seattle embarrassed the mayors of those cities when they offered to help close down the towns' many speakeasies. Earlier in 1923, IWW Locals in Portland had a lighthearted fling when they demonstrated in protest outside a well-known "soft-drink establishment." They were arrested.[33]

It would not do to deny the Wobblies their romantic heritage and their place in the revolutionary tradition. The leg-

ends are factual as often as not, and they rank among the
most exciting in the American experience. And the Wobblies
were, as they said, "true-blue" revolutionaries. They envisioned the total reconstruction of American society on a design
which they esteemed as infinitely more democratic, equitable,
and humane than what they saw around them. Perhaps the
point is that, in its nervous conservatism, America too often
dismisses its revolutionaries as bizarre by definition, forgetting
that a revolutionary, utopian streak runs through the fabric
of American history like a color through a plaid, sometimes
dim, sometimes bold, but always a part of the design.

Perhaps the fundamental error is that history has too neatly
categorized the IWW as "revolutionary studies," forgetting
that it was founded as a labor union and that it functioned
rather well as a labor union during the years before the World
War. There is, of course, a problem of what a labor union is
or should be. William D. Haywood's definition of the term
differed radically from that of Samuel Gompers. For the
IWW's most important task was its revolutionary end, the
abolition of the wage system and the establishment of "industrial democracy." The AFL, of course, had no such goal.
Under the tutelage of Samuel Gompers and the National Civic
Federation, the Federation shunned all "ultimates" and devoted itself to working-class improvement within capitalism.
Tactically, Gompers divined, the worker's lot could best be
improved through practical and immediate demands for collective bargaining, union recognition, shorter hours, higher
wages, better conditions of labor, and improved social services.
After fifty years it is obvious that the Gompers design has
become the American standard. And it is by that standard
that the question of the IWW *as a union* should be historically
considered.

It is often overlooked that the IWW was founded with the idea of unionism rather than revolution most clearly in mind. When Big Bill Haywood convened the meeting that founded the IWW in 1905, he deliberately addressed the delegates as "Fellow Workers" rather than the traditional "Comrades." And there was nothing inherently revolutionary in his keynote assertion that "we are going down into the gutter to get at the mass of workers and bring them up to a decent plane of living." [34]

The Manifesto that summoned the assembly had been concerned chiefly with outlining a Marxian analysis of the "great facts of present industry." But the authors (all of them seasoned old unionists) also noted that the IWW was not going to lose sight of the present in the brilliant glare of the ultimate revolution. For, while never losing sight of the ultimate goal, the IWW was to work for the "betterment of the working class," a task for which, all agreed, the craft-divided AFL was sorely unfitted.[35]

The founders of the IWW were committed to the industrial form of organization not only because it was the only logical way to organize a revolutionary union but also because industrial unionism was more effective from a pure and simple unionist point of view. When Father Thomas Hagerty devised the new union's internal organization (which one student has called the most comprehensive union structure ever designed), he pointed out that the first aim of the labor organization must be to "combine the wage workers in such a way that they can most successfully fight the battles and protect the interests of the working people of today in their struggle for fewer hours, more wages, and better conditions." This immediatist view was echoed practically every time a Wobbly mounted a soapbox to explain the principles of the organization.[36]

In fact, if the revolutionary rhetoric is momentarily set aside, it is clear that the IWW conducted its major eastern strikes at McKees Rocks, Pennsylvania (1909), Lawrence, Massachusetts (1912), Akron, Ohio (1913), and Paterson, New Jersey (1913), for the same pragmatic ends for which the AFL conducted its many strikes during the same period. This "bread-and-butter" facet of the Wobbly strikes was obscured by the fact that newspaper reporters found their best copy when Haywood or Joseph Ettor or Carlo Tresca told the strikers that someday they would own the factories. With a few exceptions, the press glossed over the fact that the focal issue of the strikes was not, at the moment, who owned the factories but a desire for higher wages or improved conditions of labor. The Wobbly leaders, despite their claims that even a lost strike served a positive function, actually scored a strike as a victory or a defeat on the basis of whether or not it resulted in any immediate gains. In her postmortem on the Paterson strike, Elizabeth Gurley Flynn showed that the IWW was hardly hidebound in its approach to a strike situation. "We have no ironclad rules," she stated, "we realize that we are dealing with human beings and not with chemicals. And we realize that our fundamental principles of solidarity and class revolt must be applied in as flexible a manner as the science of pedagogy." [37]

When Bill Haywood testified before the Industrial Relations Commission in 1913, the commissioners were anxious to hear about the IWW's revolutionary ideology. But Haywood wanted to talk about the IWW's unionism and to boast of the union's concrete accomplishments. He did not attempt to conceal even the reddest aspects of the ultimate revolution that the IWW visualized. But he emphasized the movement's unionist features. Commissioner Harris Weinstock at one point

asked Haywood if he did not think that it would take a long
time before the "whole world" adopted Wobbly principles.

Haywood replied that "it does not make any difference to
me if it is not for a hundred years." Surprised, Weinstock
asked what the IWW would do in the meantime.

Haywood: "The same thing we are doing now—plugging
along and taking our part in the class struggle, fighting for
better conditions and hoping to get them tomorrow, but fighting for them, if we do not get them for a century." When
another Commissioner asked Haywood what he would recommend to Congress if he were a member of the Commission,
Haywood replied that "I think I would advise to meet the
needs of the people, employment, work, such as the Government could do—reclamation, reforesting stations—such work
as would meet the unemployed; that is, just as remedial
measures." When pushed further on the same point, Haywood
told his examiners that he was before them to speak about "the
necessities of life—food, clothing, shelter and amusement. We
can talk of Utopia afterwards," he added, "the greatest need is
employment." [38]

All of which does not make Haywood a proto-New Dealer
or the IWW merely another pure and simple union. Neither
Haywood nor the union ever lost sight of their revolutionary
goal. But neither did they ever scorn whatever immediate
gains might be collected in the meantime. John Graham
Brooks, one of the IWW's few contemporary analysts who approached an understanding of the movement, saw the IWW
in yet another light. The Wobblies were indeed becoming
"practical," Brooks observed in 1913, and the reason was "almost too simple to be stated." As in any large group of bread-
winners, Brooks continued, many men of the IWW were mar-
ried and relatively well paid for steady work. These particular

members, as opposed to the footloose, were oriented to unionism rather than revolution.[39]

"On the first approach of definite responsibility" such as
the IWW found in Lawrence and Paterson, Brooks concluded,
the heretofore extreme leaders "reflect, compare, and balance."
They acted as the politician acted. In the thrill of the revolutionary moment, perched high on a platform with thousands
of militant strikers surrounding them, IWW orators mouthed
ominous and uncompromising slogans. "But, on the first as-
surance that the battle was to be won, compromise was a
necessity. With as much shrewdness as haste, the strikers took
to the ordinary bartering of practical men. As the theory
passed into a situation that must be met, they met it in the
spirit of a sensible trade union or an arbitration board—the
spirit of a wholesome opportunism." [40]

While astute, Brooks's analysis was incomplete in that he
did not realize that bread-and-butter unionism had always
been a characteristic of the IWW and not merely a belated
reaction to specific situations. Nor did Brooks seem to realize
that bread-and-butter unionism was as much a part of the
IWW rhetoric as were its revolutionary rhapsodies. In a New
York City speech of May, 1913, Haywood told his audience
that "we will take from the bosses what we can get today, and
we will hold what we can get. Then we will take more," a
statement indistinguishable from any of innumerable Gompers
perorations.[41] A declaration by Wobblies who led a strike at
Bisbee, Arizona, is almost verbatim Gompers' much-quoted
statement of principle before the 1913 Industrial Relations
Commission: "After our present demands of $6.00 for eight
hours are granted we will begin to prepare for the next step
onward, $8.00 for six hours." [42] The eulogies for Joe Hill,
Wobbly martyr executed in Utah in 1915, were based partly

on lamenting the death of a revolutionary hero but also noted that "Joe Hill lived and died for these ideas—shorter hours, more pay, more of the good things of life for workers—shelter, food." [43]

Most AFL attacks on the IWW emphasized the Wobblies' "utopian" revolutionism but others fathomed that the difference between the two organizations was *"a difference in degree, not in kind."* [44] Wobbly-AFL debates, a frequent event during the IWW's early years, generally did not center on the IWW's revolutionary program versus AFL conservatism but upon the comparative effectiveness of the two organizations in meeting the immediate demands of the workers.[45]

The IWW's brief period of prosperity between 1909 and the World War was due only in part to the organization's revolutionary appeal. An Ohio State Commission that investigated the Akron rubber workers' strike of 1913 concluded that it was the IWW's practical and effective unionism that won over the workers:

> Very few of the striking employees . . . testified that they believed in the doctrine of sabotage, but almost universally they stated that they had affiliated with the Industrial Workers of the World's organizations because they hoped, through collective action, to increase their wages and improve their conditions of employment.[46]

A Presidential Commission of 1917 came to the same conclusion, that "membership in the IWW by no means implies belief in or understanding of its philosophy. To a majority of members it is a bond of groping fellowship. . . . A very small percent of the IWW are really understanding followers of subversive doctrine. The IWW is seeking results by dramatizing evils and by romantic promises of relief." [47]

The workers who joined the IWW in great numbers during the 1910s were not, as the President's advisors implied, oblivious to the fact that the union had a revolutionary program. Bombastic Wobbly orators drove home that point in a dozen languages. But it is likewise clear that the IWW exerted a great attraction through its effectiveness as a union during a period when the AFL seemed weak and on the retreat. It is noteworthy that the IWW did not "call" any of the Eastern strikes that marked its apogee. At McKees Rocks, Lawrence, and Paterson, the IWW was summoned only after workers had walked out spontaneously and found themselves in need of guidance. In Paterson, the IWW was contacted only after the AFL's United Textile Workers had been called by the strikers only to have UTW president John Golden accused of collusion with the millowners and repudiated. The strike was a month old when Wobbly organizers Flynn, Tresca, and Haywood arrived. One observer noted that if John Golden had "come to Paterson on February 25th, undoubtedly he could have organized the workers in his union. Instead came Haywood, Elizabeth Flynn, Quinlan, Tresca—empty-handed, with neither money nor credit nor with the prestige of a 2,000,000 membership, but willing to work and go to jail." [48]

Paterson was a failure but the IWW proved its worth as a union in McKees Rocks and Lawrence. In the Pennsylvania city the Wobblies scored one of the few union victories in the steel industry between the 1890s and 1930s. In Lawrence the IWW took on a wealthy, powerful, and united textile industry willing to employ any tactics to defeat it, and the union won a complete victory. In none of the three strikes did "the revolution" play the leading role; the question on which the IWW fought the strikes was a wage cut pure and simple.[49]

Other incidents illustrate the IWW's unionist nature. Beginning in 1911, for example, the IWW press and leadership perched on the verge of launching an eight-hour movement. This not very revolutionary goal was a foremost topic in the pages of *Solidarity,* the organ of the IWW's eastern wing. The IWW later claimed that it was the threat of a Wobbly union in the Detroit automobile industry that prompted Henry Ford to introduce his famous eight-hour day. Several of Ford's advisors partially corroborated the claim.[50]

The IWW failed as a union just as it failed as a revolution. Not until the day of the Congress of Industrial Organizations would the Wobbly faith in industrial unionism be vindicated. While it adopted the IWW structure, however, the CIO rejected Wobbly radicalism and the IWW's scorn for employer recognition and time contracts. This scorn was in part based on the IWW's revolutionism. Vincent St. John, an early Wobbly leader, summed up the case when he stated: "There is but one bargain that the Industrial Workers of the World will make with the employing class—complete surrender of the means of production." [51]

But the IWW also had a practical reason for its policies. By committing the worker to his job for a specified period of time, the Wobblies argued, the union might be committing him to scab in the event that workers in a related industry went out on strike. This, for the most practical of reasons, must be avoided; no time contracts were permitted. A contemporary analyst noted another aspect of the same issue. If the union could be held together, the IWW could act more efficiently on the workers' behalf than a contract-bound union in that it could choose its own time for striking rather than waiting for a contract to expire.[52]

On a few occasions, Wobbly locals took exception to the no-recognition, no-contract policy. An IWW secretary in the

Fresno, California, agricultural district in 1916 signed an agreement to furnish men who would pick raisin grapes at 3½ cents a tray (somewhat higher than the going rate in the district) in return for IWW-supplied labor.[53] And, in the aftermath of the Paterson strike in November, 1913, there was a brief walkout, apparently in violation of an informal agreement, when a shop refused to fire a man who did not belong to the IWW. The IWW longshoremen's union in Philadelphia (which was briefly quite powerful) demanded and received a closed-shop agreement.[54]

The Wobblies' legacy to conservative American unionism has been considerable. The industrial form of organization survived through the medium of the CIO. It was the CIO's return to Wobbly-like militance after the lethargy of the Samuel Gompers and William Green AFL that renewed organized labor as a force to be reckoned with and forced further accommodations by corporate capital. But the historical issue at stake is not that these contributions have been totally overlooked. They have not. The point is that the IWW was a vital and constructive force within its milieu as well as an alternate vision of the future. Historians of American radical and labor movements too often reflect the prejudices of the American consensus in portraying those movements of which it is possible to be tolerant—the dead ones—as at best poetically futile. The IWW, at least, was a good deal more, an insight in itself as to why the Wobblies are no more. The Wobblies were not a curious aberration in their time and place. They evinced a commitment to traditional American liberties more edifying than their enemies'. They displayed a regard for law in practice which they themselves believed that they scorned. Hardly ideologues, the Wobblies were pragmatic and practical. They were buoyed by the same optimism for the future as the progressives and they shared in even the vagaries of the time. All of which is to make a point which would be downright silly if it were not so tenaciously ignored, that the Wobblies were more like their contemporaries than either party cared to admit.

NOTES

1. N.d., quoted in Harvey O'Connor, *Revolution in Seattle* (New York: Monthly Review Press, 1964), p. 34.

2. Odie B. Faulk, *Land of Many Frontiers: A History of the American Southwest* (New York: Oxford University Press, 1968), p. 275.

3. Wallace Stegner, *The Preacher and the Slave* (Boston: Houghton Mifflin, 1950), p. vii.

4. William D. Haywood, *Bill Haywood's Book: The Autobiography of William D. Haywood* (New York: International Publishers, 1929), p. 7; for similar sentiments, see Ralph Chaplin, *Wobbly: The Rough and Tumble Story of an American Radical* (Chicago: University of Chicago Press, 1947), pp. 91, 139, 347; Eugene Barnett, "Centralia: Personal Narrative," typescript in the Vertical File, Labadie Collection, University of Michigan as well as in a host of informal prefaces to essays and letters in Wobbly newspapers; Covington Hall, *Battle Hymns of Toil* (Oklahoma City: n.d.) and "Labor Struggles in the Deep South," typescript, Labor History Archives, Wayne State University; Carleton H. Parker, *The Casual Laborer and Other Essays* (New York: Harcourt, Brace & Howe, 1920); William E. Walling, *Labor-Union Socialism and Socialist Labor-Unionism* (Chicago: C. H. Kerr & Co., 1912).

5. Ralph Chaplin, "Why I Wrote *Solidarity Forever*," *The American West* (January, 1968).

6. Richard Brazier, "The Great IWW Trial of 1918 in Retrospect," typescript, Labor History Archives, Wayne State University, p. 4.

7. Parker, *Casual Laborer*.

8. Spokane *Spokesman-Review*, January 18, 1909, quoted in *Industrial Union Bulletin*, February 7, 1909. The subject of the IWW and violence is considered in detail below, chapter 4.

9. Robert L. Tyler, *Rebels of the Woods: The IWW in the Pacific Northwest* (Eugene, Ore.: University of Oregon Books, 1967), p. 47.

10. Ed Delaney and M. T. Rice, *The Bloodstained Trail* (n.p., 1927), p. 53; Elizabeth Gurley Flynn, *I Speak My Own Piece: Autobiography of the Rebel Girl* (New York: International Publishing Co., 1955), p. 95.

11. Delaney and Rice, *Bloodstained Trail*, p. 7.

12. Mary A. Hill, "The Free Speech Fight at San Diego," *The Survey* 28 (May 4, 1912): 193.

13. Fred E. Heslewood, "Barbarous Spokane," *ISR* 10 (February, 1910): 710–711.

14. Fred Thompson, *The IWW: Its First Fifty Years* (Chicago: IWW Publishing Bureau, 1955), p. 48; Flynn, *I Speak My Own Piece*, p. 94; Heslewood, "Barbarous Spokane," p. 706; Delaney and Rice, *Bloodstained Trail*, pp. 54–57.

15. Quoted in Heslewood, "Barbarous Spokane," p. 706.

16. Thompson, *The IWW*, p. 49.

17. Quoted in Heslewood, "Barbarous Spokane," p. 712.

18. Justus Ebert, The IWW in Theory and Practice 5th rev. ed. (n.p., 1937), p. 47.

19. *Chicago Daily News*, October 2, 1917; Chaplin, *Wobbly*, pp. 231, 237, 285.

20. John Reed, "The Social Revolution in Court," *Liberator*, September, 1918, p. 28.

21. "News and Views," *International Socialist Review*, April, 1910, p. 948; Mary A. Hill, "The Free Speech Fight at San Diego," p. 194; Tyler, *Rebels of the Woods*, p. 43; *Portland Oregonian*, November 28, 1911.

22. Flynn, *I Speak My Own Piece*, p. 93; a similar incident was reported in Spokane.

23. Tyler, *Rebels of the Woods*, pp. 77–78; *Seattle Daily Times*, November 8, 1916.

24. Tyler, *Rebels of the Woods*, p. 178.

25. *Industrial Union Bulletin*, May 11, 1907.

26. Ebert, *IWW*, p. 50.

27. David Mulder, letter from International Workers Defense League to Women's Clubs of California, December 15, 1913.

28. Tyler, *Rebels of the Woods*, p. 166; see also *Seattle Union-Record*, November 12, 1919.

29. Chaplin, *Wobbly*, p. 296.

30. *Sacramento Bee*, October 18, 1916; *Sacramento Union*, October 18, 1916.

31. "An Explanation by Ex-Chief of Police Hutchinson," Socialist Party of America Papers, Duke University; see also Phillips Russell, "Strike Tactics," *New Review*, March 29, 1913, p. 406.

32. "More Truth About the IWW," pamphlet, IWW collection, State Historical Society of Wisconsin, Madison.

33. *Portland Oregonian*, April 26, 30, 1923; see also *The Nation*, October 3, 1923; Tyler, *Rebels of the Woods*, pp. 204–205.

34. *Proceedings of the First Convention of the Industrial Workers of the World* (Chicago: IWW Publishing Bureau, 1905), pp. 575–576.

35. "Manifesto," *Proceedings of the First Convention;* an easily accessible source for Wobbly documents is Joyce Kornbluh, *Rebel Voices: An IWW*

Anthology (Ann Arbor: University of Michigan Press, 1964). The "Manifesto" is published on pp. 7–11.

36. Robert E. Doherty, "Thomas J. Hagerty, The Church, and Socialism," *Labor History*, vol. 3 (Winter, 1962); *The Voice of Labor,* May, 1905; see, for example, Justus Ebert, *Trial of a New Society* (Cleveland: IWW Publishing Bureau, 1913), p. 43; Elizabeth Gurley Flynn, "The Truth About the Paterson Strike," typescript of a speech delivered at the New York Civic Club Forum, January 31, 1914, Labadie Collection, University of Michigan Library.

37. Flynn, "Truth About Paterson."

38. William D. Haywood, *Testimony Before the Industrial Relations Commission,* IWW pamphlet (Chicago: IWW Publishing Bureau, 1913), pp. 50, 67–69.

39. John Graham Brooks, *American Syndicalism: The IWW* (New York: Macmillan Co., 1913), p. 215.

40. *Ibid.,* pp. 217–218.

41. Haywood, May 24, 1913, speech in New York City, quoted in William E. Walling, *Progressivism and After* (New York: Macmillan Co., 1914), p. 156.

42. Ebert, *Trial of a New Society,* p. 34; see also John MacDonald, "From Butte to Bisbee," *International Socialist Review* 17 (1916): 70.

43. Barrie Stavis, "Joe Hill: Poet/Organizer," *Folk Music,* June–August, 1964, p. 3.

44. "The Deceit of the IWW," United Cloth Hat and Cap Makers of North America, pamphlet (New York: 1906), emphasis in original.

45. Fragment of "Agreement" to debate between Thomas Flynn (AFL) and E. R. Markley (IWW), February 15, 1906, Vertical File, Labadie Collection; see also, "The History of the IWW," unidentified pamphlet, Tamiment Institute, New York.

46. "Report of Ohio Legislative Committee Investigating the Akron Rubber Strike" in James Boyle, *The Minimum Wage and Syndicalism* (Cincinnati: Stewart & Kidd Co., 1913), p. 128.

47. *Report of the President's Mediation Commission, 1917* (Washington, D.C.: Government Printing Office, 1917), p. 14.

48. Fitch, "The IWW: An Outlaw Organization," *The Survey* 30 (June 17, 1913): 81.

49. Good accounts of the IWW's great strikes may be found in the two standard books on the Wobblies, Paul F. Brissenden, *The IWW: A Study of American Syndicalism* (New York: Russell & Russell, 1919) and Philip S. Foner, *History of the Labor Movement in the United States* (New York: International Publishing Co., 1965) vol. 4, *The Industrial Workers of the World, 1905–1917.*

50. See *Solidarity* for most of 1911, for example, February 11, 1911. See also: John Spargo, *Syndicalism, Industrial Unionism, and Socialism* (New York: B. W. Huebsch, 1913), p. 43; "Program" of the Paterson Pageant, p. 23; editorial, *International Socialist Review,* 11 (February, 1911): 492;

Brooks, *American Syndicalism*, pp. 218–219; Agnes Inglis, "Reminiscences," Manuscript, July 19, 1926, Vertical File, Labadie Collection; Foner, *The Industrial Workers of the World*, pp. 389–390.

51. Vincent St. John, *The IWW: Its History, Methods, and Structure* (Chicago: IWW Publishing Bureau, n.d.), p. 12.

52. Mary B. Sumner, "Broad Silk Weavers of Paterson," *The Survey*, March 16, 1913, p. 1934.

53. *Fresno Republican*, September 8, 1916. In recent years, the remnants of the IWW have winked at the no-contract rule. The last Wobbly collective bargaining unit was in a Cleveland foundry. About 1960 the workers in the shop voted to reaffiliate with the AFL-CIO. It appears that prior to this the Wobbly local acted as a contract-making organization in the usual fashion and local activists in the labor movements referred to the Cleveland IWW's as "Wobbly pure and simplers." *Cleveland Plain Dealer*, February 14, 1965. I am indebted to Donald Murphy of Cleveland State University for information about the latter-day Wobblies of that city.

54. *New York Times*, November 22, 1913; David J. Saposs, *Left Wing Unionism: A Study of Radical Policies and Tactics* (New York: Russell & Russell, 1967), p. 156.

4

Men of Beautiful Countenance

SALT LAKE CITY newspaper readers were startled by a remarkable headline on December 31, 1916. "Plan Is Made to Poison Community with Strychnine," it read. The article which followed began in a confusing manner, with what appeared to be instructions on how to accomplish the foul deed: "Dissolve one eight-ounce bottle of strychnine sulphate in one half pint of boiling water. One or two men should prepare the poison for the entire community." Its readership by then doubtlessly intrigued, the newspaper dispelled the mystery: "This is no IWW plot but part of the instructions issued by agricultural agent of Salt Lake City, Herbert J. Webb, for destroying sparrows." [1]

Whether or not the readers of the item had a hearty chuckle over the prank, the allusion to the Industrial Workers of the World was not lost on them. During its heyday before and for a decade after World War I, the IWW had a most unsavory reputation for violence. In the popular eye, the IWW was a conspiracy of desperate villains who set fire to wheat fields, drove spikes into sawmill-bound logs, derailed trains, destroyed industrial machinery, and killed policemen. So there was nothing preposterous in the suggestion that plans to poison a "community" might be on the Wobbly agenda as well.

This reputation for violence was one of the major sources of the IWW's antisocial image, of course, and the telling issue on which the Socialist party repudiated the IWW in 1913, a significant episode for both organizations. This reputation is also a historical distortion of the worst sort, for the fact is not merely a matter of shifted emphasis but almost the diametrical contrary. During the half-decade or so preceding World War I, the IWW's central office in Chicago was dominated by the attitudes of the union's eastern or "industrial unionist" wing. This leadership, headed by the redoubtable William D. "Big Bill Haywood, did not envision or, in fact, head a violent organization. In fact, the Haywood IWW unequivocally rejected violence and often acted as a positive force for peace in the industrial disputes in which it took part; the IWW was *nonviolent* almost to a point of principle. Even the more loosely organized western wing, centering in the mining towns, lumber camps, and agricultural belts—while circumstantial evidence attributes certain depredations to individual members—was rarely violent as an organization and was censured by the central office when it hinted otherwise. And certainly the western Wobblies were no more prone to the use of violence than were the members of the AFL or any other conservative labor union.

The IWW rejected violence on grounds of both theory and expediency. Thus, as early as 1907 (the union was founded in 1905), the official organ stated that while violence "is the

basis of every political state in existence, [it] has no place in
the foundation or superstructure of this organization." [2] Wobblies visualized their union as the governing body of the
coming commonwealth which was emerging as industrialism
matured—"building the new society within the shell of the
old" as the Wobblies phrased it. Certainly there could be no
place for violence in such an organization. A Wobbly at Lawrence, Massachusetts, the scene of the IWW's greatest triumph
as a union, explained that violence was "reactionary and out of
date." [3] The union's General Executive Board in 1920 was
more explicit. No principle could ever be settled by force, the
Board argued, and what was worse, "Such methods destroy
the constructive impulse which it is the purpose of this organization to foster and develop in order that the workers may
fit themselves to assume their place in the new society." [4]

The IWW also rejected violence because the nature of the
revolution they envisioned simply did not require it. To the
IWW, the new society was to be accomplished not by an
electoral victory nor by taking to the barricades but by a general strike that would paralyze the economy and force the
employing class to hand over peacefully the means of production. Wobblies were nearly mystical when they spoke of the
power of the workers who "folded their arms."

Strikes for immediate gains were also rehearsals for the
eventual general strike and therefore also need not be violent.
Violence was "useless," a Lawrence Wobbly said, "as we have
only to quit work and the whole capitalist machinery is at a
standstill."[5] Big Bill Haywood and other Wobbly leaders
seemed never to tire of telling the workers that they had only
to remain away from work in order to win their disputes.
Ralph Chaplin, once second only to Haywood in the Wobbly
organization, later recalled that he had rejected violence as

a viable tool before 1913. "Squirrel guns," he concluded, would be of little help to auto workers in establishing a union and that, after all, was the IWW's goal.[6]

In addition to their theoretical rejection of violence, the eastern Wobblies eschewed its use on grounds of expediency. Unarmed workers could not hope to match force with wealthy employers, armed police, and militia. The General Executive Board's white paper on violence in 1920 stated that "history shows that violence breeds official government violence and the workers lose their cause immediately." William D. Haywood cautioned the strikers at Lawrence to "stay in your houses; don't let the police or the soldiers provoke you into a fight." He realized that, as the journalist Robert Bruyere wrote in 1918, violence invariably started with and favored the best prepared, and the employers and police were the best prepared.[7]

Moreover, Haywood and some other Wobblies had an inarticulated conception of the now-familiar idea that nonviolence often frustrated the adversary into the use of violence, and the public's comparison of peaceful workers with violent employers would channel the tide of public opinion to the workers' cause. This was exactly what happened at Lawrence and at Spokane, and the experience confirmed Wobblies in their policy. In both cities the brutality of the police and the resultant public protest were of major importance in accounting for the IWW's victories. At Paterson, New Jersey, Haywood made his position clear when he shouted to a mass meeting of workers that their power rested in their folded arms. "You have killed the mills; you have stopped production; you have broken off profits. Any other violence you may commit is less than this, and it will only react upon yourselves."[8]

Other Wobblies placed equal emphasis on the efficacy of positive nonviolence. When Joe Ettor, the union's general organizer, arrived in Lawrence to take command of the strike in early 1912, he cautioned. "By all means make this strike as peaceful as possible. In the last analysis, all the blood spilled will be your blood. And if any blood is spilled, it will be on the hands of the millowners, for they will be responsible for it." [9]

Critics of the Wobblies, both contemporary and subsequent, have often singled out William D. Haywood as the spirit of violence in the IWW, pointing to his past as a leader of the violent Western Federation of Miners and his trial for the murder of former Idaho governor, Frank Steunenberg. Although it is difficult to tell so from some histories, Haywood was acquitted of the Steunenberg murder, and the available evidence suggests that Haywood's violent past in the WFM disillusioned him with the utility of violence rather than confirmed him in the use of it. The southern Wobbly leader, Covington Hall, told of a conversation with Haywood after Big Bill had arrived from delivering a speech in Grabow, Louisiana, a lumber-mill town. The news arrived of a riot in Grabow and Haywood was greatly disturbed. "I don't know why something like that is always following me around the country," Haywood said. Hall observed that Haywood seemed nervous for the rest of the day and left abruptly after his last lecture.[10]

Haywood continued to speak of revolution during his Wobbly period, of course, but it was bloodless revolution to which he referred. "The world is turning against war," he said not too presciently in 1913. "People are sickened at the thought. Even labor wars of the old type are passing. I should never think of conducting a strike in the old way. There will never be another Coeur d'Alene, another Cripple Creek

[WFM strikes that more closely resembled small wars than industrial disputes]. I for one, have turned my back on violence. It wins nothing. When we strike now, we strike with our hands in our pockets. We have a new kind of violence— the havoc we raise with money by laying down our tools. Our strength lies in the overwhelming power of our numbers." [11]

So much for advocacy. In practice the IWW was consistent, spurning the use of violence in its strikes and sometimes functioning as a positive force for peace in labor disputes. While they were not directly concerned with wages, hours, or conditions, the free speech fights which the IWW waged between 1909 and 1911 at Missoula, Montana; Fresno and San Diego, California; Spokane, Aberdeen, and Kansas City were industrial disputes in that they were directed at IWW's right to organize. All were characterized by nearly complete nonviolence on the part of the Wobblies and sometimes vicious brutalities on the part of authorities and mobs of citizens.[12] The Wobblies' adherence to peaceful demonstration and civil disobedience could have served as a model for Gandhi and Martin Luther King, Jr.

In McKees Rocks, where the workers at the Pressed Steel Car Works struck in 1909, the IWW actively served as a pacifying force. The strike had been called spontaneously, and its early stages were marred by considerable violence on both sides; several strikers and at least one Pennsylvania State constable were killed. According to the *Nation*, the strikers had 3,000 men under arms, probably an exaggeration but indicative of the temper of the town.[13] When the IWW entered the strike, the violence immediately ceased. An apocryphal tale attributes the change to a Wobbly dictum that for every striker killed a policeman would be killed, but there is no evidence for the story. In fact, the IWW introduced its policy of no violence and the authorities conformed. Several neutral observers said that they had never seen less violence in such a large strike.[14]

At Lawrence, Massachusetts, in 1912, the situation was similar. The strike was spontaneous, in response to an unannounced wage cut in January. As the various spinning and weaving shops walked out independently, threads were cut, windows smashed, and power belts slashed in order to prevent nonstrikers from working.[15] On another occasion violence erupted when police turned firehoses on a group of pickets and they retaliated by throwing ice at the police. But that was all before the IWW took charge of the strike!

Summoned by the tiny Franco-Belgian Wobbly local in the town, organizer Joseph Ettor immediately warned the workers that they must shun violent tactics and observe absolute nonviolence. One incident seemed to give the lie to Ettor's public policy. Shortly after he arrived, Lawrence police made several raids including one at a shoemaker's shop next door to a house where Ettor received his mail. They found several caches of dynamite. The millowners and some newspapers were quick to blame the IWW, but the Wobblies denied any knowledge of the explosives. They quietly launched their own investigation when a rumor spread that the Boston Hearst paper was already on sale in Lawrence with the news of the discovery before the police had actually made the raid. It was then revealed that the dynamite had been wrapped in old copies of a trade magazine, the *Undertaker's Journal,* from one copy of which the subscriber's name had been imperfectly removed. He was John J. Breen, who had been county coroner, and was at the time of the strike a member of the Lawrence School Board. After Breen's arrest it developed that William Wood, principal owner of the American Woolens Company, Lawrence's largest mill, had recently made an unexplained payment of money to Breen. Wood was not molested and Breen was fined $500—mild punishment, the Wobblies thought, but they were gratified to be cleared of the charge.[16]

On another occasion Ettor acted positively to avoid provocation by a company of militiamen. On January 28, 1912, he was leading a protest march through the retail business district when a group of militia suddenly blocked the strikers' path. Thinking quickly, Ettor led the group up a side street and rapidly disbanded them.

Hardly did the IWW bring violence into the city, a reporter wrote at the time, the IWW stemmed it in the face of the workers' frustration, the employers' provocations, and the militia's irresponsibility.[17] A local Protestant minister remembered five years later that the IWW leaders were "men of beautiful countenance," perhaps an overstatement. They believed in "the beautiful philosophy of nonresistance," he wrote.[18]

While Lawrence provides the best example of IWW nonviolence in action, neutral observers testified to the same fact in innumerable instances. A woman in Butte, Montana, was surprised at the tenacity with which the Wobblies refrained from responding in kind to violent provocations.[19] Several government prosecutors and even agents of the Federal Bureau of Investigation agreed.[20] Another woman testified in court that she had heard speeches by all the major Wobbly agitators in the Pacific Northwest including "Red" Doran, James Rowan, James P. Thompson, and Elizabeth Gurley Flynn, and had never heard any of them "advocate or teach crime. They are strictly opposed to violence." [21] A police chief in Colorado reported that an IWW meeting which he attended discussed

the question of what they should do if they were attacked by
a mob nearby. Much to the sheriff's surprise, the Wobblies decided that if the mob came, they would leave rather than
promote violence.[22] A Los Angeles police captain wrote that
he was ashamed to have done the "dirty work" of the employers in attempting to provoke the Wobblies to violence.
"These Wobblies are better men than we are," he said. "They
show better self-control." [23]

William B. Wilson, Secretary of Labor under Woodrow
Wilson, ruled that the constitution of the IWW did not show
that the union advocated violence or force.[24] The American
Civil Liberties Union, which defended the Wobblies indicted
under the Sedition Act of 1918, stated that "the common
charge of violence to achieve the organization's purpose *has
not been proved in a single trial.*" Not a single fact "has been
proved against the organization which could not be proved
against any aggressive A. F. of L. Union." [25] The Federal
Council of Churches, after investigating the disturbances in
the Colorado coal fields in 1927, in which the IWW was involved, marveled at the union's avoidance of violence.[26] The
Immigration Bureau wrote after a long examination of the
IWW that only *hints* of violence could be found in IWW
writings and concluded that even in regard to "sabotage," the
IWW's meaning was "not altogether clear or well defined." [27]

In fact, the IWW's concept of sabotage was better defined
than that of its accusers, and the Wobbly definition bore only
casual relationship to the popular notion of the destruction
of property. Sabotage was a relatively new word describing an
ancient, virtually natural practice. Labor's first official use of
the term appears to have been in a report by Émile Pouget
and Paul Delassalle to the Congress of the *Confédération
Générale du Travail* which met at Toulouse in 1897.[28] The

word was a device which approximated the meaning of an old Scots phrase, *ca canny,* which meant to work like the farm boys who were often brought to the Glasgow docks in order to break longshoremen's strikes. In 1889, for example, the Glasgow dockers struck over their employer's refusal to grant a twopenny per hour raise, and farm boys were imported to do the dockers' work. At a union meeting, the secretary observed that the employers had expressed perfect satisfaction with the farmers' work although it was clear to everyone that the strike-breakers were incompetent. They could not walk the deck of a pitching ship properly and they often dropped what they were carrying. "The conclusion is obvious," the union decided, "return to your jobs and do the same quality work, ca canny, take it easy; only those fellows used to fall in the water now and then; you needn't go as far as that." [29] The dockers returned to work, "took it easy," and soon won their raise.

"Sabotage" meant much the same thing. It was coined from *sabot,* the clumsy wooden shoe worn by the French peasants who, themselves, often served as strikebreakers. The workers were told to return to work and walk as if they were wearing *les sabots.* Some critics maintained that the term referred to throwing a *sabot* into machinery but it is a contrived explanation.[30]

To most Americans, sabotage meant simply damaging machinery, and they based their fear of the IWW on this imperfect understanding. To the IWW, the word meant considerably more. Violence was one form of sabotage. Another was simply going slowly, *ca canny.* The French phrase was *"à mauvaise paie—mauvaise travail";* the Wobblies called it "striking on the job." As Elizabeth Flynn wrote in a Wobbly pamphlet on the subject, "sabotage means either to slacken up and interfere with the quantity, or to botch in your skill and interfere with the quality of capitalist production so as to give poor service. It is something that is fought out within the walls of the shop." She added, although the phrase was ignored, "sabotage is not physical violence, sabotage is an internal industrial process. It is simply another form of coercion." [31]

A third type of sabotage was obstructionist. It consisted in carrying out all orders literally, regardless of the consequences. Many industries, in response to laws demanding safety devices, published long lists of inconvenient rules which, if broken, disqualified an injured man from compensation. The saboteur's reaction was to follow literally all the cumbersome rules that no one ever intended to be obeyed. The employers usually soon agreed to compensate for injuries suffered in violation of the rules. The usual illustration cited occurred in Austria in 1887. When a railroad coupler was caught between two freight cars and mutilated, the stationmaster was disciplined and fined because he had not observed several regulations. The master telegraphed orders to other stationmasters that they were to see that all rules be followed to the letter. Within twenty-four hours the trains were piled up and the railroad's national governing board voted to free stationmasters of all responsibility for accidents due to infringements of rules. The same tactic was used effectively by Italian railroad workers in 1905. [32]

A fourth form of sabotage was "big mouth," what the French called, *La bouche ouverte*. It consisted simply of publicity, telling the truth to the customer. In 1908 a Parisian chef was fired for refusing to cook decayed meat. The Paris cooks' syndicate then revealed to customers how crayfish soup was made not of crayfish meat but of crayfish and lobster shells which had been left on plates and were finely powdered and sprayed with carmine. "Venison," they revealed, was beef steeped overnight in condiments. In 1910, bank clerks in Paris surreptitiously gathered information about dishonest or dubious transactions in which their employers were involved and made their collection known to the employers on the occasion of a grievance.[33] An IWW waiters' strike in New York City was settled in the workers' favor when the union threatened to make public a list of hotels which maintained unsanitary kitchens or served adulterated, impure, or spoiled food.[34] Inexplicably, a progressive analyst of the Wobblies was quite upset at what he called "this delicate cruelty of exact truth-telling recommended by the IWW" when he heard a Wobbly tell clerks and retail vendors to "get together, study the foods, candies, and every adulterated product. Study the weights and measures, and all of you tell the exact truth to every customer." [35]

Another form of sabotage involved benefiting the customer at the expense of the employer. Thus, wineshop workers instructed to dilute wines should secretly abstain from doing it. Cooks given margarine to use in products sold as butter-baked should use so much margarine that they became just as rich and expensive as if butter had been used. Grocery clerks must never shortweight customers although they might be told to do so. Apothecary clerks should always recommend the least expensive variety of a prescribed drug and they must not omit any high-priced ingredient although such might be their employer's policy.[36]

Sabotage, then, stood for considerably more than the burning of crops and the destruction of machinery. Yet this latter definition won broad and sole acceptance. Even John Spargo, who inordinately emphasized the single violent variety, attested to the fact that few people who most loudly damned the use of sabotage really understood the term or could even pronounce the word.[37]

The Wobblies did advocate sabotage, distribute pamphlets describing its employment, and in 1914 officially recommended that its speakers spread the word. Nor were they always circumspect about specifying the nonviolent varieties. Mabel Dodge lumped Haywood with Emma Goldman and Alexander Berkman as saying that "they believed in killing" and that "they advocated it when it was possible." She added that, "of course, the IWW's led by Bill Haywood, Carlo Tresca, Elizabeth Gurley Flynn, and Giovannitti advised sabotage for industrial machinery no matter what the risk might be to human life." [38] Mrs. Dodge was, as usual, guilty of some sensationalism in her parlor analyses. Flynn, at least, explicitly warned against destructive sabotage in her writings on the subject.[39] Arturo Giovannitti, who translated Émile Pouget's *Le Sabotage* into English, went to great pains in a lengthy introduction to disagree completely with the Frenchman's advocacy of damage to property. Giovannitti stated that he could support only the nonviolent varieties of the tactic.[40] In a conversation with George Perkins of the "steel trust," Giovannitti condemned the planting of dynamite by workers as well as by employers. He told Perkins that when he said "an eye for an eye," he meant, "a dishonest day's work for a dishonest day's pay." [41]

How, then, did the IWW get its bloody reputation? Primarily it was a reputation foisted upon the union by its enemies: the employers it struck; the cities whose anti-street-speaking ordinances it defied; AFL unionist rivals; anti-unionist politicans; and the reformist wing of the Socialist party. The IWW's brief age of prosperity was an era when unions were widely suspect in the United States, and the IWW represented the most militant sort of unionism. The most distorted account of Wobbly activities could be widely disseminated and believed in such an atmosphere. As Richard Brazier, a prominent Wobbly, remembered: "The IWW, of course, never did have a 'good press' and we were more or less accustomed to being made the whipping boys for something we knew nothing about." [42]

An antiunionist public's credulity was only one way by which the IWW's reputation was fixed. On various occasions, agents provocateurs were employed by the union's enemies. It is likely that the single speaker, out of hundreds, who advocated violence on the Wobblies' open platform at Paterson, New Jersey, in 1913 was hired to do so.[43] Harvey O'Connor recalled an incident in Everett, Washington, where, when an IWW speaker began to preach violence, he was pulled from the platform by "fellow" Wobblies.[44] Agents provocateurs were widely employed in the western lumbering areas. A reporter for the *New York Post* wrote that owners of lumber mills frankly admitted to him that "the peculiar reputation for violence and lawlessness which has been fixed upon the IWW was largely the work of their own ingenious publicity agents." [45]

In a case in which the IWW was accused of sabotage, an admitted "professional witness" for the prosecution impeached his own testimony with so many contradictions that even the friendly local newspapers were upset.[46] At a Wobbly trial at Sacramento in 1918, two Wobblies, Elbert Coutts and John Dymond, testified that the California IWW had been engaged in incendiarism since 1912. But, as William Preston notes, the two were coconspirators according to their own confession and were "by all odds, disreputable witnesses." [47]

The IWW's implication in many trials for murder and other violent crimes has served to perpetuate their unsavory reputation. Ironically, in virtually every case the IWW was acquitted. William D. Haywood is always remembered as the defendant in the famous Steunenberg murder case, but the fact that he was acquitted for lack of evidence is widely ignored. Wobblies Joseph Ettor and Arturo Giovannitti were involved in another sensational murder case in connection with the 1912 Lawrence strike but they, too, were acquitted. Over a hundred Wobblies were, of course, convicted of "sedition" during World War I but virtually every subsequent student of the affair has interpreted that trial as at best a shabby affair.[48] In fact, as the historian who studied the question most closely concludes, there was absolutely "no case of an IWW saboteur caught practicing sabotage or convicted of its practice." [49] The imprisoned Wobblies were more pungent: "The liberals, bless their saccharine souls . . . usually preface a five-line plea for our release with twenty lines making clear that they do not under any circumstances believe in violence. There they sound like intellectual poltroons absolving themselves from an imaginary crime." [50]

The IWW was roundly condemned for its defense of the McNamara brothers who pleaded guilty to bombing the *Los Angeles Times* building in 1910, and the brothers' ignominy was extended to the Wobblies. However, in their defenses of the McNamaras (who were not Wobblies but Democrats, members of the AFL, and Roman Catholics) the Wobblies were always scrupulous to point out that they did not approve of the act of violence, but could sympathize with the desperation that drove the men to their action. Frank Bohn, the leading IWW theorist, stated that the brothers were misguided only in the way in which John Brown was misguided: they selected the wrong tactic. "The hearts of the McNamaras were right. It was their heads which were in error." [51]

The Wobbly newspaper, *Solidarity,* asked: "Must we weakly apologize for those of our kind who occasionally strike back under great provocation? The capitalist sowed the wind and reaped a little zephyr of a cyclone. . . . Let the blood be upon the hands of our masters."[52]

Finally, the IWW was susceptible to being tarred as a violent organization owing to the statements of some members from the union's western wing. Individual Wobblies who were clearly not agents provocateurs did make violent statements. An anonymous Wobbly told John Graham Brooks that although they refuse "to put the public to serious risk, . . . we can manipulate the machinery easy enough—from the engines to the track, we can put big trouble and big expense onto the managers." [53] Appearing before the Industrial Relations Commission, IWW leader Vincent St. John asked, albeit rhetorically: "Why should we hesitate about destroying property? It isn't ours. Instead, the employer uses it to our disadvantage whenever he can. Furthermore, he isn't careful about our property, our physical and mental power. He sends us into the mines as children, without a semblance of an education, speeds us up, underpays us, wears out our bodies, and then, without a thought of our well-being, throws us upon the scrap heap or abandons us to the poorhouse when we are no longer useful." [54] In another instance, the *Industrial Worker* (the organ of the IWW's western wing) wrote that some loggers had threatened to drive spikes into logs bound for the sawmills. "Terrible," the paper commented in mock horror. "No good, honest, Christian, gentlemanly logger would do anything like that. It isn't good for the mill saws." [55]

Despite the fact that no Wobbly was ever convicted of driving a spike into a log or igniting a wheat field, it is reasonable to conjecture that these statements had their parallels in practice. The antisocial attitudes of many of the western Wobblies were similar to those of the Western Federation of Miners from which they derived and whose violence Big Bill Haywood had rejected. Former Wobblies recall that members were sometimes recruited involuntarily. (A common tactic was to require the purchase of a "little red card" as a "pass" to ride the freight trains.) It is quite possible that several waves of fires in the California agricultural regions such as that around Fresno in 1917 were the work of individual Wobbly incendiaries.[56] An old West Coast Wobbly, Clarence Langford, recalled that while the early Wobblies practiced no sabotage, and the eastern Wobblies always frowned upon it, "the hops and lumber bosses proved to be so vulnerable in the pocketbook that it was decided to employ that weapon." [57] And another, on his way to a job as a cook in a transient camp where scabs were attempting to break an IWW strike, wrote a friend that "there's going to be lots of fun here slinging hash in a camp. The lumberjack won't need any salts when I go to work." [58]

On the other hand, it bears repeating that despite dozens of prosecutions and the investigative powers of a dozen states, the Federal Bureau of Investigation, the Immigration Bureau, and the Justice Department, *no Wobbly was ever proved to have committed an act of violence.* Former workers in the western agricultural regions, well insulated by the statute of limitations, recall witnessing no violence of IWW origin. The nearest thing to sabotage recalled by Carl Keller, currently the IWW's secretary-treasurer, was the practice of jamming a hay bailer; it did not damage the machinery but merely stalled it temporarily so that the workers could enjoy an unauthorized rest break.[59]

It is noteworthy that all the American writers on sabotage, Wobbly and anti-Wobbly alike, found it necessary to go to European examples to describe the methods, including the nonviolent ones. Not that there were no American examples, but these were not many. It is ahistorical to blame the IWW for practices which workers had performed long before the IWW was founded and have continued to perform since its demise. As John Spargo, a scathing critic of the IWW, wrote in 1913, sabotage was a practice that "so corresponded with an almost universal instinct of the oppressed workers." [60]

On balance, the IWW must be characterized as a nonviolent union. The rare Wobbly statements advocating violence were aberrations, not the norm. The *Industrial Worker* was suspended by the central office for its article on driving spikes into logs.[61] Finally, the only evidence which characterized the IWW as violent was verbal and must be viewed in that context. Like all radicals in American history and, perhaps, like all men not in power who would like to be, individual Wobblies spoke and wrote a great deal and not always prudently. They wrote and spoke many things for the purpose of attracting attention (just as they organized Salvation Army-type brass bands in the Pacific Northwest). A senator from Montana reported after responding to local accusations of IWW violence that the trouble consisted solely of "a lot of intriguing and seditious talk." [62]

The IWW cannot be exonerated from responsibility for the occasional violent utterances of its Western members; historical figures and movements must be judged by their words as well as their deeds. However, the IWW's contemporary accusers (and some subsequent historians) might have paid closer heed to those deeds (and to the words of antiviolence which are far more numerous than the statements to the contrary). It is appropriate to recall the theme of John Millington Synge's *Playboy of the Western World,* that there is a great gap between a gallous story and a dirty deed.

Fierce posturings are, while unfortunate and often ungainly, not sufficient evidence to convict. It was the American Woolens Company that planted the dynamite at Lawrence. It was a Roman Catholic priest who maintained that the socialist is "the mad dog of society and should be silenced, if need be by a bullet." [63] It was an eminent Boston lawyer who maintained that the militia at Lawrence "should have been instructed to shoot . . . the way Napoleon did it. The strikers should have been shot down." [64] And it was a Paterson newspaper that called for new cemeteries in town, "the first graves to be filled with Haywood and his crowd." [65] These, too, were fierce posturings, but posterity has not affixed a reputation for violence to textile companies, Roman Catholic priests, Boston lawyers, or New Jersey editors because of them. Yet the evidence which accounts for the IWW's reputation was no more substantial; it was based on words.

Historians today would not as a rule react adversely to the idea of labor unionism. But to regard the IWW as a force for violence in American industrial history is to be shackled by the antiunionist encumbrances of the past. The contemporaries of the Wobblies who affixed the reputation for violence to the IWW knew that it was a labor union which they were attacking. If labor historians realize the same, the Wobblies can be studied for what they were, rather than for what their enemies maintained they were.

NOTES

1. *Salt Lake Telegram,* December 31, 1916.

2. *Industrial Union Bulletin,* May 11, 1907.

3. *Boston Evening Transcript,* February 10, 1912.

4. Quoted in John S. Gambs, *Decline of the IWW* (New York: Columbia University Press, 1932) pp. 223–225; other Wobbly resolutions to the same effect may be found in *Solidarity,* May 22, 1920, June 9 and September 15, 1923; *Defense News Bulletin,* May 4, 1919.

5. *Boston Evening Transcript,* February 10, 1912.

6. Ralph Chaplin, *Wobbly: The Rough and Tumble Story of an American Radical* (Chicago: University of Chicago Press, 1948), p. 146.

7. Robert Bruyere, "The IWW," *Harper's Weekly,* July, 1918, p. 253.

8. *The Survey* 27 (March 30, 1912): 205; "Program of the Paterson Pageant," June 7, 1913, Labadie Collection, University of Michigan Library, Ann Arbor.

9. Quoted in Justus Ebert, *The Trial of a New Society* (Cleveland: IWW Publishing Bureau, 1913), p. 49.

10. Covington Hall, "Labor Struggles in the Deep South," typescript, Labor History Archives, Wayne State University, p. 156.

11. *The World's Work,* 26 (1913): 417.

12. The best narrative account of the free speech fights is Philip S. Foner, *History of the Labor Movement in the United States* (New York: International Publishing Co., 1965), vol. 4, *The Industrial Workers of the World, 1905–1917,* pp. 172–214.

13. *The Nation,* August 26, 1909.

14. Paul Kellog, "The McKees Rocks Strike," *The Survey,* August 7, 1909, p. 664.

15. Fred Beal, *Proletarian Journey: New England, Gastonia, Moscow* (New York: Hillman-Curl, 1937), pp. 40–41.

16. William D. Haywood, *Bill Haywood's Book: The Autobiography of William D. Haywood* (New York: International Publishers, 1929), p. 252; Beal, *Proletarian Journey,* p. 49; *Lawrence Sun,* May 14–17, 1912; *Solidarity,* June 22, 1912; *Report on Strike of Textile Workers in Lawrence, Massachusetts,* 62nd Cong., 2nd sess., Senate Document No. 870, p. 39; Foner, *The IWW,* p. 334; Paul F. Brissenden, *The IWW: A Study of American Syndicalism* (New York: Russell & Russell, 1919), p. 289; G. D. H. Cole, *The World of Labour* (London), p. 149.

17. Mary K. O'Sullivan, "Labor War at Lawrence," *The Survey* 28 (April 6, 1912): 73.

18. *New York Times,* October 15, 1917.

19. Fanny Bixby Spencer to Nicholas Steelinck, August 11, 1920, Steelinck Collection, Labor History Archives, Wayne State University.

20. William Preston, *Aliens and Dissenters: Federal Suppression of Radicals* (Cambridge: Harvard University Press, 1963), p. 104; U. S. Attorney Clay Allen to the Attorney General, July 6, 1917, Department of Justice File 186701-49-6; Bruyere, "The IWW," *Harper's Weekly*, July, 1918, p. 254.

21. *State of Washington* v. *Pat Cantwell*, 119 Wash. 665, No. 16811, "Statement of Facts," p. 38, quoted in Donald S. Barnes, "The Ideology of the IWW," Ph.D. diss., University of Washington, 1962, pp. 2, 158.

22. "An Explanation by Ex-Chief of Police Hutchinson," unpublished manuscript, Socialist Party of America Collection, Duke University Library.

23. Quoted in Gambs, *The Decline of the IWW*, p. 45.

24. *Annual Report: Secretary of Labor of the United States, 1920* (Washington, D.C., Government Printing Office, 1920), pp. 78–79.

25. "Memorandum Regarding the Persecution of the Radical Labor Movement in the United States" (New York: National Civil Liberties Bureau, 1919), p. 4.

26. Gambs, *Decline of the IWW*, p. 151.

27. Preston, *Aliens and Dissenters*, p. 101.

28. John Spargo, *Syndicalism, Industrial Unionism, and Socialism* (New York: B. W. Huebsch, 1913), pp. 147–148.

29. Quoted in Andre Tridon, *The New Unionism* (New York: B. W. Huebsch, 1913), p. 39.

30. Emile Pouget, who should have known, subscribes to the former explanation. J. A. Estey, *Revolutionary Syndicalism* (London: P. S. King & Son, 1913), p. 96; Walker C. Smith, *Sabotage* (Chicago: IWW Publishing Bureau, 1913), pp. 1–2.

31. Elizabeth G. Flynn, *Sabotage* (Chicago: IWW Publishing Bureau, n.d.), p. 5.

32. Tridon, *New Unionism*, pp. 43–50.

33. Tridon, *New Unionism*, pp. 43, 48–49.

34. Spargo, *Syndicalism*, p. 42.

35. John Graham Brooks, *American Syndicalism: The IWW* (New York: The Macmillan Co., 1913), p. 141; see also Moses Oppenheimer, "Direct Action and Sabotage," *New Review* 1 (January 25, 1913): 113–115.

36. Tridon, *New Unionism*, pp. 49–50.

37. Spargo, *Syndicalism*, p. 140.

38. Mabel Dodge Luhan, *Intimate Memories* (New York: Harcourt, Brace and Co., 1936), vol. 3, *Movers and Shakers*, p. 88.

39. Elizabeth Gurley Flynn, "The Truth About the Paterson Strike," typescript of a speech delivered at the New York Civic Club Forum, January 31, 1914, Labadie Collection, University of Michigan Library.

40. Émile Pouget, *Sabotage*, trans. Arturo Giovannitti (Chicago: C. H. Kerr & Co., 1913).

41. *The Survey*, 31 (November 8, 1913): 167; *ibid.*, 31 (August 2, 1913): 561.

42. Richard Brazier, "The Great IWW Trial of 1918 in Retrospect," typescript in the IWW Collection, Labor History Archives, Wayne State University, p. 4.

43. Partick L. Quinlan, "The Paterson Strike and After," *New Review* 2 (January, 1914): 29; Elizabeth Gurley Flynn, *I Speak My Own Piece: Autobiography of the Rebel Girl* (New York: International Publishing Co., 1955), pp. 148–149.

44. Harvey O'Connor, *Revolution in Seattle: A Memoir* (New York: Monthly Review Press, 1964), p. 37.

45. *New York Post*, February 16, 1918.

46. *State of Washington* v. *Edward Aspelin* and *State of Washington* v. *Alfred Petilla*, quoted in Donald M. Barnes, "The Ideology of the Industrial Workers of the World" (Ph.D. diss., Washington State University, 1962), pp. 145–146.

47. Preston, *Aliens and Dissenters*, p. 136.

48. The best account of the wartime prosecutions is Preston, *Aliens and Dissenters.*

49. Eldridge Foster Dowell, *A History of Criminal Syndicalism Legislation in the United States* (Baltimore: Johns Hopkins Press, 1939), p. 36. Dowell's conclusion, based on an exhaustive study of the laws under which the IWW was prosecuted for sabotage among other offenses, is convincing. His original work, upon which the book is based, was a Ph.D. dissertation at Johns Hopkins University, a massive compendium of data running over 1,300 pages.

50. Harrison George, quoted in *The Truth About the IWW Prisoners* (New York: American Civil Liberties Union, April, 1922), p. 17.

51. Frank Bohn, "The Passing of the McNamaras," *International Socialist Review* 12 (January, 1912): 400.

52. *Solidarity*, January 4, 1912.

53. Quoted in Brooks, *American Syndicalism*, p. 141.

54. Quoted in *The Survey*, vol. 32 (May 30, 1914). In justice, a contradictory (and more widely expressed) Wobbly viewpoint on the subject should be cited. When asked if the IWW damaged property, a Wobby replied: "Won't we be taking them over one of these days, and what sense would there be in destroying what is going to belong to us?" Quoted by Bruyere in *Harper's Weekly*, July, 1918, pp. 250–257.

55. *Industrial Worker*, December 26, 1912.

56. Preston, *Aliens and Dissenters*, p. 132.

57. Clarence Langford to the author, November 26, 1968.

58. T. J. O'Connell to G. A. Roberts, February 17, 1917, University of Washington Archives, quoted in Barnes, "The Ideology of the IWW," p. 145.

59. Interviews by the author with Carl Keller, Fred Thompson, and several unnamed Wobblies, Chicago, August 6, 7, 9, 1965; Richard Brazier to the author, May 18, 1966; Carl Keller to the author, July 17, 1963; Fred Thompson to the author, March 6, July 24, August 1, 1965.

60. Spargo, *Syndicalism,* p. 157.

61. Robert F. Hoxie, *Trade Unionism in the United States* (New York: D. Appleton and Co., 1917), p. 144.

62. Quoted in Preston, *Aliens and Dissenters,* p. 95.

63. James O'Neal, "Catholicism and Socialism," *Wayland's Monthly* 2 (April, 1915).

64. Harry Emerson Fosdick, "After the Strike in Lawrence," *Outlook* 101 (January 12, 1913): 340.

65. *Paterson Press,* March 29, 1913.

5

Our Vote-Getters Fail
in Getting Votes

OF ALL THOSE who have misrepresented the nature of the
IWW, none did it so cynically as the right wing of the Socialist
party in 1912 and 1913. "Cynical" because the Socialists had
ample opportunity to apprise themselves of realities and must
have acted consciously and deliberately where others wagged
their heads out of ignorance or misadvice. There was another
difference. Of all those who misrepresented the character of
the IWW, only the Socialist party paid for its error.

While successful socialist parties have long been familiar in
Europe, none has ever developed in the United States. The
closest to one was the Socialist party of America during the
first two decades of the twentieth century. Pieced together
during 1900 and 1901, the SPA had a brief but exciting heyday. Growing slowly but steadily in membership and votes
during the first years of the century, the party enjoyed a
quick spurt of electoral successes beginning in 1910. Com-

mentators of all political persuasions predicted that it would soon become a major political force.

The SPA's first electoral victories in 1910 surprised the newly elected Socialist officials as well as their defeated opponents. And 1911's successes reduced the previous year's victories to insignificance. When the results of both spring and fall elections were tabulated, party officials announced that the party had elected 56 mayors, 305 aldermen and councilmen, 22 police officials, 155 members of school boards, and 4 poundkeepers. Victor Berger of Milwaukee had already taken his seat as the nation's first Socialist congressman.[1]

Then in 1912 the national ticket polled nearly a million votes, about 6 percent of the total, despite the fact that both Democratic and Bull Moose parties ran on "progressive" reform platforms. It was a considerable gain, fully 481,043 votes more than the party's presidential vote of 1908. The number of elected local Socialists had risen from 450 in 1911 to about 1,000.[2]

Contrary to partisan hopes, however, 1912 was not the dawn of a new era but the apogee of socialist success. With the elections of 1913 the SPA lost many of its previous gains. Socialist mayors, aldermen, and poundkeepers found themselves displaced by Republican, Democratic, Progressive, or "fusion" tickets formed for the express purpose of defeating the "red menace." In 1916 the SPA's presidential ticket polled only 581,113 votes, an especially disappointing decline from 1912 inasmuch as women suffrage amendments in many states had enlarged the electorate considerably. Proportionately, the 1916 candidate's share of the electorate was about half that which Eugene V. Debs drew in 1912.[3] Although the party experienced a revival during the World War, it was clear by 1920 that the sanguine predictions of a major party future had been pipe dreams. Except for a few pockets of local strength such as Milwaukee, the SPA's "golden age" was over.

The Socialist party of 1910–1913 was not an "extremist" party. Its leadership, program, and dominant tenor were, rather, reformist. While party propaganda sometimes paid lip service to the ultimate goal of socialism, most candidates emphasized their "immediate" program: minimum wages and maximum hours legislation, antitrust laws, political democratization, clean government, and so on. In practice, the SPA often appeared to be no more than a third "progressive" party. Many pointed out, for example, that the SPA and Bull Moose platforms of 1912 were almost indistinguishable.

The party's moderate character was largely the work of Victor Berger's virtually autonomous Social Democratic party of Milwaukee, whose views the national party adopted by 1912. The SDP was the most successful of all the SPA's local components. By 1913 the city had a Socialist mayor, a Socialist city council, several Socialist state legislators, and Berger had already spent the first of several terms in Congress.[4] Berger's argument in party councils was that a party without power was ludicrous, that socialists must establish the legitimacy of their governance. Therefore, the SPA should consider the winning of elections as its primary immediate goal. To win elections it was necessary to be opportunistic, and in the United States this meant the necessity to emphasize the party's essentially progressive immediate program and play down its revolutionary end. The American electorate had indicated that it wanted reform. Berger argued, but the voters were patently not amenable to revolutionary fire-eating. Finally, Berger added, capitalism could be reformed to death by means of gradual, ameliorative legislation.[5]

Duly noting the SPA's moderation in practice, historians and political scientists have generally explained the party's rapid rise and fall in terms of the "third-party thesis." The thesis, developed variously by several scholars, was perhaps most succinctly phrased by William B. Hesseltine. "By voicing grievances and by proposing panaceas," Hesseltine wrote, "third parties have exerted significant influence upon the policies and programs of major parties. In a curiously anomalous manner, third parties have bolstered the traditional American two-party system. . . . Often third parties voiced dissents and made sufficient headway at the polls to force the attention of the political managers of a controlling group. Frequently, third parties were the vehicle through which a new idea or policy was launched and tested. When a new proposal met a favorable reception it was adopted by a major party," and the third party, having served its function, ceased to exist as a viable political force.[6]

This had been the fate of the populists during the 1890s when the Democratic party adopted the free-silver panacea. And, on the face of it, as historians have argued, this was the fate of the moderate SPA.[7] As the Socialist party grew and won votes, apparently because of its demands for moderate change, progressives within the major parties observed and became more outspoken and demanding themselves. Then, when after 1912 Woodrow Wilson's "New Freedom" accomplished much of the progressive program, the SPA quickly fell apart. According to the "third-party thesis," the party's pioneering reformist program had been effectively pilfered and it no longer had a functional reason to exist. The World War with its accompanying reaction merely administered the coup de grâce.

The "third-party thesis" is a valuable tool for understanding American political development, and it is not at all irrelevant to the Socialist party of America. In some respects, however,

the thesis is inadequate. For instance, the SPA did not decline
uninterruptedly after 1912. Rather, the party enjoyed a renais-
sance during World War I as a vehicle of antiwar sentiment
long after the "triumph of progressivism" and the SPA's assumed functional irrelevance.[8] The party's wartime success
was due to something more than the mild reformism which
the major parties could easily absorb, namely, a radical militance on the war issue. This fact provides the key to understanding the SPA's apogee between 1910 and 1913 as well.

The "third-party thesis" assumes that the SPA was nothing
more than a reformist party become redundant when the major
parties expropriated its program. In fact, there had always been
more to the party than its immediate demands. While the moderate reformists dominated policy-making, they were constantly challenged within the party organization by a large
"revolutionist" faction. The revolutionists derisively referred
to the reformists as "slowshulists." They sneered at the notion
that capitalism could be reformed or legislated out of existence
and they felt that to deemphasize the party's revolutionary
nature was nothing less than a betrayal of principle. Capitalism could only be overthrown by revolution which, while not
necessarily violent, meant no compromise with the masters.
Translated into tactics, the revolutionist viewpoint attributed
little value to winning elections. To be sure, socialist office-
holders could play a role in the revolutionary process. They
could, for example, prevent legislation adverse to the working
class. And SPA officials would extort reform legislation from
the capitalist-owned municipalities, states, and, perhaps, even
the federal government. The party could also serve an important educational purpose. Through its campaigns the SPA
could transmit sound knowledge to the workers and educate
them in the necessity for revolution. All the better if the party

won its elections; their victories would attract the workers' attention.[9]

The point of all this was that socialism could not be effected by elections. If elected socialist officials showed signs of approaching a majority, the master class could be expected to suppress them through other than elective means.

The revolutionists maintained that the labor union was the agency of revolution. Therefore, while electioneering should by no means be ignored, the party's chief interest should be in encouraging and aiding the labor movement.

For the militant socialists of the early 1900s, the "labor movement" meant the Industrial Workers of the World. Already skeptical of the value of winning elections on reformist "false pretenses," the SPA's revolutionist wing was attracted by the IWW's color and efficacy and they urged that the party hitch its fate to the union.

With this the reformists heartily disagreed. Many of the moderate socialists such as Berger and Max Hayes of the International Typographers Union held positions of some power within the AFL and looked forward to the day when socialists would win the Federation. The IWW was anathema to most of the AFL leaders as a "dual union" and, therefore, an obstacle to the reformist ambition of converting the Federation's non-socialists.

Even more objectionable in terms of the reformists' electoral ambitions was the IWW's preachment of sabotage. While the word had many meanings and the IWW viewed it primarily as "striking on the job" by means of a slowdown, sabotage in popular connotation meant flaming wheat fields, wrecked machinery, and, in general, the destruction of life and property. To the reformists it was obvious that the SPA would not win votes among moderate Americans interested in prudent change so long as the party was associated with such an organization.

Finally, progressives friendly to the Socialist party urged the reformist leaders along. Charles Sprague Smith wrote to Morris Hillquit, the reformist leader of the New York City Socialists, that the party was "a very important element in the progressive movement" and that "it is imperative that [the SPA] be under the control of the intelligent, cool-headed, historically-informed, spiritually-consecrated men" like Hillquit rather than the revolutionists.[10]

It was on the issue of the IWW that revolutionist and reformist wings of the party clashed, with the latter emerging victorious. After the electoral successes of 1910 and 1911, the reformists were convinced that they were on the verge of an era as a major officeholding party and that only the SPA's informal association with the Wobblies stood in their way. They joined the issue over William D. Haywood. "Big Bill" was a member of the party's Executive Committee and also the best-known Wobbly leader. As such, he was the favorite of the revolutionist wing and the symbol of union-party association.

In March 1912, the reformists made a false start toward repudiating the IWW when the Yuma, Arizona local introduced a motion to recall Haywood from his position on the grounds that he had made certain statements deprecating political action. However, when the Lawrence textile strike ended in success shortly thereafter, enhancing Haywood's popularity among radicals, the resolution was stillborn.[11] At the 1912 convention, however, the reformists amended the party constitution calling for the expulsion of all advocates of sabotage and violence. After the near-million vote of November 1912, the reformists were heartened on the basis of the new amendment to recall Haywood again. While most partly regulars had been enthralled by the large vote that year, the reformist leaders had predicted up to two million votes and publicly attributed the "poor" showing to the party's continuing identification with the Wobblies. If the Socialist party was to move ahead, then, it was essential that those socialists whom Berger called the "cranks" and "impossibilists" be harried out of the party. Haywood's recall was moved once again and this time approved by a party referendum in which only about 20 per cent of the party membership bothered to vote.[12]

According to the reformist strategy, their repudiation of the IWW should have led to the further growth of the SPA. The progressive daily press responded precisely as the reformists had hoped it would. Especially gratifying was the *New York World*'s statement that the Socialist party could now "honestly appeal to public opinion as a party that recognizes the rules of orderly government and rejects the theory that the lawless shall gain power by intimidation and lawlessness."[13] The *Metropolitan Magazine* congratulated the "thousands upon thousands of good citizens" within the party who could not tolerate the "Haywood element." Now that the SPA's true character was revealed, the *Metropolitan* continued, the party would "immediately attract the real Progressives."[14] In fact, the "new" SPA attracted no one. The year 1912 proved to be not the harbinger of a glorious era but the apogee of SPA success.

The party had actually enjoyed its largest membership before the election of 1912 when, in May of that year, there were some 135,000 members. Membership declined to 100,000 after the adoption of the antisabotage amendment, a development the reformists anticipated, with the welcome exodus of the "Haywood element." But the decline was not over. During the four months after Haywood's recall, membership dropped precipitously to 80,000. Thereafter followed a slow recovery but it was already apparent to some that there was no "golden age" imminent; it had already come and gone.[15]

Reflecting the same decline, reverses in local elections in 1913 all but wiped out the victories of 1910, 1911, and 1912. Some of the most important cities previously won by the Socialists returned to Republican, Democratic, Progressive, or fusion control.[16] In addition, official and unofficial socialist newspapers found themselves suddenly without their usual financial support. Within the few months before August 1913, such seemingly well-established papers as the Chicago *Daily Socialist,* the *Coming Nation,* and the *Cleveland Socialist* shut down their presses. The *Washington National Socialist* merged with the *Appeal to Reason.*[17]

In complete control of the party by 1916, the reformists accomplished Berger's long-standing wish to nominate a moderate for president in the person of the journalist, Allan Benson. Benson polled only 3 percent of the total vote compared to Debs's 6 percent in 1912. After the election, the party's decline continued. The brief revival during and just after World War I (with nearly a million votes for Debs in 1920 when he campaigned from Atlanta Prison, where he was jailed because of opposition to the war) was a last gasp.

What had happened was that the reformist wing had seriously misinterpreted the source of the party's membership and votes. Their recall of Haywood and repudiation of the IWW was based on the premise that "progressive" voters responding to the SPA's "immediate program" had given them the victories between 1910 and 1912. They had concluded that should the revolutionist aspects of the party's program be played down, even more progressives would rally to their standard. Their error is more easily excused than that of later analysts who accepted and perpetuated the reformist analysis.

In retrospect it is clear that the SPA's support was of another sort altogether. With the notable exception of Milwaukee (where the large German population's old-country socialism made the city unique), the SPA flourished best between 1910 and 1913 in those areas where it was most militant, and languished where the reformists framed party tactics. It was in the revolutionist areas as well that the party suffered its worst losses beginning in 1913 when the reformists repudiated revolutionism. While they would not have appreciated the distinction, the SPA revolutionists were inadvertently the better electoral tacticians. As one of them wrote in 1909, "Our 'practical' politicians not only compromise our principles, but prove to be impractical. Our vote-getters fail in everything, even in getting votes." [18]

The correlation between revolutionist militancy and electoral success was evidenced as early as 1908. In the presidential election that year, the greatest gains over 1904 were made in states where the revolutionists controlled the party and framed the tactics, emphasizing the party's revolutionary end. Pennsylvania, Michigan, Minnesota, Idaho, and Colorado Socialists claimed the greatest rates of growth; all were states with militant party organizations. In the words of a revolutionist at the time, in states "which had gone all-out to win the reformist votes," the party did miserably, losing out badly to the progressive Democrat, William Jennings Bryan.[19]

The trend was even more marked in 1910 and 1911. A detached observer, Robert F. Hoxie, wrote in the *Journal of Political Economy* that states such as Pennsylvania and Ohio (where pro-Wobbly revolutionists controlled the SPA organ-

ization) scored the party's greatest gains. Moreover, the strong-
est counties within those states were those where the revolutionists were most vociferous.[20] States with a proportionate decline included the reformist-controlled states of Florida (more
than 50 percent loss), Tennessee, Wisconsin, Maryland, Dela-
ware, and Oregon.[21]

Most significant, the Socialist party did especially well in
areas where the IWW was active. Whether or not the IWW
officially opposed political action, most members did vote. The
reformist Colorado Socialist, Adolph Germer, attested to the
fact that the SPA membership in his state was often synony-
mous with the IWW.[22]

In Lawrence, Massachusetts, Haywood pointed out, only 15
percent of the workers had the vote before the IWW-led strike
but, thanks to the Wobblies, "since the strike, we have taken
into the Socialist party as many as one hundred members at
a meeting." [23] The reformist leader of the Massachusetts SPA,
explaining the party's poor showing in the state in 1912, admitted that the one bright spot was Lawrence where the party
"increased its vote very much." He added that "had the same
ratio been maintained throughout the state, we should have
had about 20,000," which was 80 percent higher than the actual
figure.[24] The Massachusetts party's gubernatorial nominee, a
social gospel Protestant minister, called upon socialists to recognize that the election taught that SPA support of the IWW
was the way to electoral success in the future.[25]

The 1913 elections in New Jersey and Ohio illustrated the
same point. While the party's statewide vote in both cases was
lower than it had been in 1912, the party gained considerably
and almost won in Paterson and Akron where the IWW had
recently been active.[26] Before the Wobbly-led strike in Paterson, the reformist New Jersey SPA had been able to muster

only some 1,650 votes in the city, but at the municipal election of 1913 the SPA mayoralty candidate received 5,155 votes, only 2,000 fewer than the victorious anti-Socialist fusion candidate. In adjoining boroughs, the SPA also gained. Their vote in Passaic increased by 500. Haledon voted Socialist, and North Haledon elected three Socialists to the borough council. Wobbly-Socialist Patrick Quinlan excoriated the national party for failing to exploit the "splendid opportunity" that IWW-inspired militance had created. "At the moment when the entire resources of the state organization should have been thrown into the Paterson strike," Quinlan wrote, the reformists "stood apathetically on one side and left it to the silk workers to demonstrate their fine class solidarity and intelligence." Thanks to the IWW "the silk workers had learned the lesson of class solidarity and the necessity of carrying that solidarity into the political field," but the anti-IWW reformists had failed to cooperate.[27]

Butte, Montana, provides the best case study of the IWW's relationship to the Socialist party's electoral success. In April 1911, the party elected almost the entire city administration. The mayor, Lewis Duncan, was in practice quite moderate (as, inevitably, were all local Socialist officials) but publicly subscribed to revolutionist principles and often spoke at IWW meetings. One reporter wrote that all eight elected Socialists in Butte were "firm believers in the principles of industrial unionism, and were supported alike by Socialists and IWW men." [28]

Four years later, after Haywood's recall, Duncan and the other Socialists were turned out of office despite a reasonably successful term. Duncan, by this time drifting with the party toward reformism and shunning his old Wobbly cronies (he had fired several from the city payroll), explained his defeat on the grounds that "the spirit of the people of Butte, Montana, has been crushed by the brutal exercise of the tremendous economic and political power of the local Rockefeller interests." [29] Nonsense, the revolutionists retorted. They noted that the Rockefeller interests had always been present in Butte and had never hesitated to exercise their economic and political power. Yet, a Wobbly observed, Duncan had had no trouble in defeating those interests in 1911, although at that time he had run against an anti-Socialist fusion ticket. (In 1915 the election was a four-way race among the SPA, the Democrats, the Republicans, and the Progressives, but the Socialists drew only 27 percent of the total vote.) The reason for the reversal in Butte, it was clear, was the wholesale desertion of the party by Wobblies and other revolutionists after the SPA had repudiated them.[30]

Wobbly withdrawal from the Socialist party was not, of course, the sole cause of the post-1912 decline; the IWW was not itself large enough to have such an effect. More important was the fact that, before 1913, Wobbly militance had won considerable support for the Socialist party from among non-Wobblies, even middle-class voters. The circumstance that the IWW was inevitably and unqualifiedly condemned by newspaper editorialists, city governments, police, employers' associations, campaigning politicians, and chambers of commerce has obscured the fact that the IWW often rallied considerable public opinion to its side during its strikes and free speech fights.

The IWW's practice of nonviolence won the admiration of some middle-class observers. Even the newspapers of Paterson, New Jersey, which had vilified the union during the strike of 1913, grudgingly conceded the strikers' good behavior when the strike was over. Other witnesses lent similar testimony.

The union often won public opinion to its side when it exposed the sometimes scandalous treatment it received at the hands of the authorities or the employers it fought. The brutality of the police against IWW prisoners in Spokane in 1909 and San Diego in 1912 swung much public opinion to the side of the Wobblies. In the former case, at least, a favorable public opinion probably was responsible for the IWW's victory. The exposure of the dreadful conditions under which the textile workers of Lawrence and Paterson worked was a by-product of the strikes in those cities in 1912 and 1913.

The IWW knew well the value of a favorable public opinion and developed many ways of cultivating it. One of the most ingenious was their practice of sending the children of a strike-torn town to be cared for in other cities. The exoduses (employed in both Lawrence and Paterson) had a practical purpose in that they relieved the union's badly strained strike funds. In addition, the IWW claim that the children's safety was in danger from irresponsible militia and police was certified at least once by the blundering police of Lawrence who attacked mothers and children on the train platform and then attempted to exonerate themselves by jailing the parents on grounds of neglect. That event probably marked the turning point of the Lawrence strike.

While the union's aim in all this was simply to win the strike or the free speech fight at hand (just as the SPA's primary aim was to win elections), their agitation also benefited the Socialist party by winning voters to the party that they saw as allied to the IWW. Far from holding the Socialist party back, as the reformists believed, the IWW–SPA alliance was one key to its success. The revolutionists who supported that alliance were indeed the superior practical politicians, and the party's post-1912 decline had little to do with the "third-party thesis."

Rather, the reason for the decline is rooted in the reformists' dissolution of that informal alliance.

The Socialist party enjoyed its two most successful periods when a militant and not a compromising attitude prevailed in party councils: the first between 1910 and 1912 when the party was informally allied with the militant IWW, the second during World War I when the party adopted a program of militant opposition to the war.

This is not to say that a militant Socialist party of America could have withstood the powerful conservative strain in American political behavior (or the stern reaction of World War I) and become a major political party. Nor is this to frame a principle for application to radical political movements in general. It is to say simply that the Socialist party of the early twentieth century failed because its tacticians adopted a diametrically incorrect tactical policy, an irony in the sense that the reformists were political opportunists before they were anything else.

Many revolutionists continued to urge a reversal of strategy after 1913 but, despite the party's obvious decline, they were ignored. A few reformists, however, did realize the error. In late 1913 a frustrated reformist comrade from Alliance, Ohio, wrote to the national office lamenting the state of the party in his town. In 1910, he wrote, the SPA had no organization in Alliance after three years of agitation and the distribution of about 40,000 pieces of reformist literature. In 1913, after three more years, the situation was about the same. "We have modelled our platform after . . . Milwaukee and have found that the old parties are only too glad to use it and make fools of the Socialists."

The reformist information officer answered the letter, suggesting that "you might have put a little more of the revolutionary purpose of socialism into the program." Perhaps recalling that he had been one of the leading agitators for disposing of the "Haywood element" a year before, he added, on second thought, "I do not believe that would have changed the situation materially." [31]

Even Victor Berger, the individual most responsible for the reformist strategy, came to change his mind. In 1918, himself by then a militant on the question of the war and denied his seat in Congress because of his stand, Berger wrote: "I am beginning to believe that the IWW (or some labor organization that will succeed it but will inherit its matchless spirit) is destined to take the place of the American Federation of Labor in our country and fulfill the mission in which the American Federation has failed." [32] Berger's change of heart, of course, came rather too late.

NOTES

1. "Annual Report of the Secretary of the Socialist Party: January 1 to December 31, 1911," *Socialist Party Monthly Bulletin*, January, 1912.

2. "National Office File," Socialist Party of America Collection, Duke University Library.

3. *American Labor Yearbook, 1917–1918*, pp. 336–337.

4. See David A. Shannon, *The American Socialist Party: A History* (New York: Peter Smith, 1955) or Ira Kipnis, *The American Socialist Movement: 1897–1912* (New York: Columbia University Press, 1952).

5. Berger's argument is well-described in Shannon, *American Socialist Party* and Kipnis, *American Socialist Movement*.

6. William B. Hesseltine, *Third Party Movements in the United States* (Princeton: Van Nostrand Co., 1962), pp. 3, 13.

7. H. Wayne Morgan, *Eugene V. Debs: Socialist for President* (Syracuse: Syracuse University Press, 1962), p. ix, is quite explicit: "the party's successes proved [that] . . . the mission of minor parties in American history has been to force major parties to accept the least radical portions of their programs."

8. James Weinstein, "Anti-War Sentiment, and the Socialist Party, 1917–1918," *Political Science Quarterly* 74 (June, 1959): 215–239.

9. The best description of the revolutionist wing's ideology is in Ira Kipnis, *American Socialist Movement*.

10. Charles Sprague Smith to Morris Hillquit, May 18, 1908. See also Walter Weyl to Hillquit, November 4, 1908, both in the Hillquit Papers, State Historical Society of Wisconsin, Madison.

11. *Socialist Party Monthly Bulletin,* March and April, 1912.

12. Mary B. Sumner, "Parting of the Ways in American Socialism," *The Survey* 29 (February 1, 1913): 627.

13. Quoted in *The Survey* 29 (March 29, 1913): 909.

14. Quoted in "Danger Ahead!," *New Review* 1 (August, 1913): 676.

15. "National Office File," SPA Collection, Duke University; see also *The Party Builder,* June 28, 1913.

16. See Morgan, *Eugene V. Debs;* Kipnis, *American Socialist Movement;* and Shannon, *American Socialist Party*.

17. "Danger Ahead!," p. 674.

18. William E. Walling, "Socialist Gains and Losses in the Recent Election," *New Review* 1 (February 18, 1913): 180.

19. Arthur Jensen, "Come on Up, Wisconsin!," *Seattle Socialist,* January 16, 1909; see also *Seattle Socialist,* December 19, 1908.

20. Robert F. Hoxie, "The Socialist Party in the November Elections," *Journal of Political Economy* 20 (March, 1912): 207–211; Hoxie, "The Rising Tide of Socialism: A Study," *Journal of Political Economy* 19 (October, 1911): 611, 613.

21. Walling, "Socialist Gains and Losses," p. 180.

22. Adolph Germer to Keir Hardie, March 18, 1913, Germer Papers, State Historical Society of Wisconsin.

23. *Metropolitan Magazine,* August, 1912; see also *Socialist Party of America: Proceedings of the National Convention, 1912,* p. 100.

24. W. Lathrop Raasch to John M. Work, November 10, 1912, "Socialist Party File," SPA Collection. See also *International Socialist Review* 17 (February, 1917): 507.

25. Rev. Roland D. Sawyer, "The Socialist Situation in Massachusetts," *New Review* 1 (January 25, 1913): 117–118.

26. Frank Bohn, "Voting, Fighting, Educating!," *International Socialist Review* 14 (December, 1913): 363.

27. Patrick Quinlan, "The Paterson Strike and After," *New Review* 2 (January, 1914): 31–33 and "Glorious Paterson," *International Socialist Review* 14 (December, 1913): 355–357.

28. Jack Keister, "Why the Socialists Won at Butte," *International Socialist Review* 12 (June, 1911): 733.

29. Lewis J. Duncan, *The American Socialist,* April 10, 1915.

30. Lowndes Maury, "What Is the Matter with Butte?," *International Socialist Review* 15 (May, 1915): 684–685.

31. John J. Scholtes to Carl D. Thompson, November 6, 1913, SPA Collection; Thompson to Scholtes, November 7, 1913, SPA Collection.

32. Quoted in Thomas W. Gavett, *The Development of the Labor Movement in Milwaukee* (Madison: University of Wisconsin Press, 1965), p. 129.

6

It's Not the Same IWW

THE IWW is still around. When the union celebrated its fifti-
eth anniversary in 1955, Dan Wakefield visited the Wobbly
Hall in New York and wrote down his impressions for *Dissent*.
What Wakefield found he called the "Haunted Hall," a few
old seamen and other workers who clung to the IWW as a
bond of camaraderie and passed their hours by swapping reminiscences about the union's Periclean Age.[1]

The Wobblies' national headquarters on North Halsted
Street in Chicago is also haunted. The office is located on the
second floor of a shabby store building. When the weather is
warm, Mexican teen-agers gather nightly outside the building,
lean against the window or parked automobiles, and, engrossed
in their conversations, never even notice the few people who
wander in and out.

Entering the Wobbly Hall's upstairs means traveling forty
years in a few steps. The walls are decorated with faded murals,

Wobbly slogans, and sepia photographs, some of which depict the union's former, more prosperous headquarters. The rear half of the office is filled with bookcases, files, and stacks of old records. In the front are a few desks cluttered with canary-colored second sheets, a dozen easy chairs and sofas, folding chairs, a few old-fashioned clumsy-looking typewriters, and two or three adding machines on cast-iron stands, all but one dusty and unused. There is not a piece of furniture in the office of later vintage than the twenties save one anachronistic gray vinyl sofa of the waiting-room type to which visitors are politely directed. The IWW's finances are precarious. It requires a campaign each year to publish the organization's tabloid monthly, *The Industrial Worker.* Despite a modest goal of $3,000 in 1967, the campaign had to be extended when not even half had been mustered at the deadline date.

Carl Keller and Fred Thompson, the most active of the older Wobblies, are most gracious with visitors. They answer questions with imagination and enthusiasm and, at times, there is a glimmer of the revolutionary fervor of the "old days."

There are younger members too. Not surprisingly, the largest IWW local in 1967 was in Berkeley. But, in Chicago at least, the young Wobblies are the source of the union's tragedy rather than its hope. They are not real Wobblies as Secretary-Treasurer Keller is quick to tell you. Most of them seem to have served some university time; a few completed their degrees and some are dropouts. At first glance they might be expected to belong to one or another of the new radical youth organizations. In fact, they are far less substantial than most of those in "the movement."

They are the New Left's lumpen. Formally they qualify for IWW membership in that they are workers for their sustenance. But they are neither unionists nor organizers and that is the crux of the matter. There is, of course, little resembling unionism in the IWW of the sixties anyway, and these young Wobblies are in the organization because they are romantics. The Wobbly legend (both its true and mythical parts) appeals to them. They know nothing of the old IWW's hard-nosed practicality and industrial unionism, only Joe Hill's challenging songs and the apocryphal tales of how the IWW dealt with Pinkertons by hanging them on meat hooks in refrigerator cars.

One small group of the Chicago Wobblies affects the ways of the storybook anarchists. They live in a reconverted stable secreted in the middle of a tenement block near "Old Town," Chicago's more garish version of Greenwich Village. The place could be a Zefirelli set for Puccini's *Bohème* if it were scrubbed up a bit and the mimeograph machines replaced by apolitical accouterments. The floors are littered with handbills and stickers for pasting on windows and billboards. Their slogans, disappointingly, are neither profound, inspiring, nor even very clever. "Lyndon Johnson is a Turd," for example, is a long way down from "Bread . . . and Roses Too!" and the folk poetry of the old IWW.

Their ethic is a weird amalgam of adolescent posing, bitter alienation, and a tiny smattering of anarchist ideology. Alienation is complete. The young Wobblies shun all cooperation with Students for a Democratic Society and the peace movement in Chicago. One might never have heard of Vietnam in the building.

Whether or not Carl Keller knows of his young members' fantasies, he does not like the New Wobblies and does not hide his feelings. He fidgets through the meetings, which the younger members dominate, speaking angrily and impatiently when he speaks at all (usually to clear up a procedural point). "I only come to make a quorum," he growls, and again, to a visitor after a meeting, "I don't know how you stood it; it makes me sick."

Fred Thompson, a formally uneducated but worthy scholar who wrote a fiftieth-anniversary history of the IWW, does not seem to notice. Thompson brings new meaning to the word "loquacious" and enjoys the meeting as a chance to discuss Wobbly and world affairs. It is a social occasion for him and for Carl Keller's pleasant wife who, claiming to be an anarchist, explodes, "Why doesn't the government do something about it?" when someone mentions the latest Mississippi atrocity.

The monthly meetings of the Chicago local are held at what Keller is quick to point out is the *semi*official Solidarity Bookstore, run by the younger members. In addition to mail orders in anarchist literature, the store's chief business is the sale and repurchase of used comic books. Its customers are the Spanish-speaking children of the neighborhood. The shop has suffered its share of harassment and was forced to move twice during the past year. It was an inexcusable action. Perhaps the young Wobblies are not very "respectable" but neither is the neighborhood where they are located. The sale of used comic books may be somewhat ludicrous as an activity for "dangerous anarchists." But one has only to see the beaming faces of the eight-year-old customers as they rummage through the pile for one they haven't seen (all the while reading as many free as they can) to realize that the Solidarity Bookstore has served a small function in which Mayor Richard Daley's crowd is apparently uninterested.

For the sake of the IWW's romantic heritage, it would have been better if they had left the scene with the bang that characterized their short career, perhaps in the cataclysm of the Great Red Scare which almost did kill them. The tragedy of the IWW's feeble longevity is like that which A. E. Housman painted for the athlete who grows flabby and stiff with the memory of past glories lingering before his eyes.

American radical groups have a way of defying the laws of natural selection. The Socialist Labor party limps along, its irrelevance dramatized by the fact that the best part of its *Weekly People* is the "text" from the work of Daniel De Leon, who died in 1914. The Communist party wheezes and puffs its way to an occasional titillating headline. The IWW is different only in that its case can be mourned. The Wobblies have bequeathed a worthy heritage to American radical and unionist alike. The whimper with which the union survives is a cruel parody that daily grows more agonizing. When Dan Wakefield wrote about the New York Wobblies ten years ago, he suggested that when the habitués of the "Haunted Hall" died, the IWW would die too. Unfortunately, Wakefield was wrong. Sustained by its new members, the "New Industrial Workers of the World" will probably limp along and an already distorted past will be twisted even more. Judging from Carl Keller's feelings about the "New Wobblies," he probably wishes that Wakefield's prediction were correct.

It is accurate to say that it was World War I that did in the IWW. The popular hysteria released by wartime patriotism and tacitly encouraged by Wilson's government found one of its favorite targets in the Wobblies. So far as the Wobblies were concerned, the Espionage and Sedition Acts of 1917 and 1918 were aimed especially at them. About 1923, a Wobbly pamphlet pointed out that the belligerents in the war, including the United States, had released all spies, dynamiters, and men charged with armed insurrection except for about fifty-nine men who remained in American prisons. Forty-three of these were Wobblies convicted of sedition on the sole basis

that they held paid-up "little red cards." [2] Ten years after the
armistice, when the consensus of a disillusioned American public was that American entrance into the war had been a sad
mistake, some Wobblies who had the misfortune to claim the
same thing in 1917 and 1918 were still in prison for their
prescience. Such facts only confirmed the IWW suspicion that
the government's motive for imprisoning them had, in the
first place, been more to destroy the union than the organization opposed to the war. Bill Haywood remained convinced
until he died that Samuel Gompers had initiated the wartime
raids of Wobbly offices. [3]

Whatever the motivation, the World War I persecutions had
four significant effects upon the IWW. [4] First, the methodical
prosecution destroyed, imprisoned, or dispersed the leadership
of the union. The Wobblies had always taken great pride in
their claim that "we have no leaders . . . we are all leaders"
but the wartime trials illustrated just how important to the
union their leaders actually were. Bill Haywood's defection to
Moscow while convicted and out of prison on appeal was especially disturbing. It had been Haywood who had called most
vociferously for all to stand together and to accept the unjust
penalties that the government was distributing. He had been
the Wobbly symbol to the rank and file, and his "desertion,"
as it was called, was a traumatic experience for the organization. Moreover, other men who might have taken Haywood's
place were, like Ralph Chaplin, in prison or, like the western
leader, Frank Little, had been lynched.

A second effect of the wartime trials was related to the first:
the dispersal of the membership. Not only the union's leaders
were tried; the government also prosecuted and convicted
many rank and filers. While this had the effect of imprisoning

many, it frightened others away from the organization, for the convicts had not been tried on the basis of any alleged specific acts but on the basis of their membership in the IWW.

Third, the war provided the catalyst that marshaled and intensified a hostile public opinion. What sentiment the IWW had won to its side during strikes such as Lawrence by revealing the truth about squalid working conditions was soon dissipated in the wartime fever. As even George Creel, Wilson's former information manager, wrote in 1919, "Just as every untoward incident was credited to the German spy system, so was every disorder, every manifestation of unrest ascribed either to the IWW or the Bolsheviki." [5] Thus, there were few demurrers when the trial of a hundred Wobblies, dealing with 17,500 counts, and compiled into 40,000 pages of typewritten testimony, ended with the jury returning a verdict of guilty after deliberating one hour and then receiving the judge's congratulations.[6] One local Wobbly trial ended with the foreman announcing his verdict of guilty and appending his statement, above the applause of the gallery, with: "Now, no one can say we're not loyal!"

A fourth and quite significant effect of the war on the IWW was that the government's repression completely transformed the organization and, to some extent, the *raison* of the union. Walter Lippmann had written in 1913 that it was always difficult to define exactly what the IWW was because the union "changes faster than most men can think." [7] In adapting to the government trials, the IWW changed quickly and irrevocably between 1917 and 1920. The prewar IWW is best defined as an industrial union in the East and a sort of haphazard association of industrial guerrillas in the West. During the war, the IWW was compelled to regroup itself into a committee for the defense of the scores of indicted Wobblies. Its wartime propaganda is indistinguishable from that of the American Civil Liberties Union, which also helped to defend the Wobblies. Contrary to the hysterical accusations that they sabotaged the war effort, the wartime IWW stood constantly on the defensive, exerting all its energies in the attempt to keep its members out of prison and to free by legal means those already in. Literally, there was no time for sabotage.

The IWW had attempted to adapt itself to wartime conditions even before the trials began. While the organization remained officially opposed to the war, other adaptive steps were taken. Sabotage propaganda, never much more than propaganda, was discontinued almost immediately after the United States entered the war. Haywood stated that the IWW Central Office ordered the cessation of the more militant antiwar propaganda as well.[8]

There were various accommodating editorial changes in Wobbly literature such as "The Little Red Songbook." Songs that might be misconstrued were deleted in the new editions. Several interesting changes appeared in Vincent St. John's history of the IWW. The controversial statement, "the question of 'right' and 'wrong' does not concern us," was dropped completely. The phrase, "an armed truce," between the classes became "only a truce" in the 1919 editions of the book. " 'Sabotage' is used to force the employers to concede the demands of the workers" became "a more favorable time [is] awaited to force the employers," etc.[9]

The most significant aspect of these changes is not that the IWW was willing to accommodate itself to society—this had always been the case—but that the IWW that made these changes fundamentally changed itself. The union no longer spent its energies inciting, organizing, directing, and financing industrial strikes. Speakers, organizers, propaganda, and

monies were all poured into legal defense. It was inevitable
that the unionist aspects of the IWW should suffer, and while
the IWW still exists, the *union* never recovered. Richard
Brazier wrote to a friend describing the day on which he and
Ralph Chaplin were released from Fort Leavenworth. "I re-
member Ralph Chaplin telling an FBI man after we were all
released . . . , 'Well,' said Ralph, 'we are still here and the
IWW is still here.' The FBI man said, 'But it's not the same
IWW.' " Brazier continued, "No, Tom, it wasn't and it never
was again. They had used all the forces of federal and state
governments to crush us and they had succeeded, but it took all
their strength and power to do it." [10]

The leaders of the postwar IWW were not the same as those
of the "golden age." Ralph Chaplin remained with the organization briefly after his release but soon drifted away. Vincent
St. John lived until 1929 but, while retaining membership, had
virtually nothing to do with the IWW. Justus Ebert drifted
into the AFL where he utilized his literary talents as the editor
of a union journal. William E. Trautmann and Arturo Giovannitti also became active in the conservative branches of the
labor movement. Joseph Ettor lived quietly in California
where he owned a small vineyard at the time of his death.
Frank Tannenbaum, an IWW martyr but never really a leader,
became one of the nation's leading scholars of Latin American
history and a professor at Columbia University. Many of the
other Wobblies found at least a temporary home in the Communist party.[11]

The new Wobbly leaders were of a different sort. Harrison
George, an old Wobbly in the Communist party during the
twenties, commented that the IWW's new departure was "an
effort to dodge revolutionary struggles" which, in a sense, was
true.[12] The IWW was in no condition to do anything else; it

was tired. One charade performed to veil the fact that the IWW was winning no more industrial strikes was the organization's pretension that the revolution was coming along inexorably and the IWW should concentrate upon preparing its members for the difficult task of managing the factories that would soon be their own. The new emphasis was, in effect, a reversal of the old unionist activism and was the logical outgrowth of the "defense committee" character of the IWW during World War I. Another writer's revised edition of Ebert's *The IWW in Theory and Practice* stated that "the ideals of the IWW are such as to encourage and require a study of industry in all its phases. It has given a new interest to technology, as a result, that cannot fail to be of far-reaching value to the new society coming." [13] That was written in 1937. As early as 1921, however, Wobblies were urged to "make a technological study of each industry, with the aid of experts" so that when the time comes, the workers will be prepared.[14] An organizing pamphlet for lumber workers, printed in the early twenties, was chiefly concerned with a technological explanation of the lumbering industry.

The IWW became introspective and exclusive in its dotage. The concern with self-preservation, which Robert Michels described, afflicted both the SPA and the IWW. Max Eastman wrote in 1921 how "we have been a little saddened of late years to see the rigidity and lethargy of age creeping over the IWW. It seems as though all organizations which do not achieve within fifteen years the purpose for which they were formed begin to be more interested in themselves than they are in their purpose. That instinctive gregarious loyalty which made them possible in the beginning makes them stiff and complacent and useless in the end." [15]

Eastman detected the introspection which the IWW had

developed. What he did not detect was that the World War I prosecutions had put the IWW under the control of the western wing by attacking and dispersing the more visible eastern leaders. What Sherman claimed happened in 1906, De Leon in 1908, Debs somewhat later, and the reformist socialists from 1910 to 1913, actually did take place as a result of the wartime trials, namely, the "bummery's" capture of the IWW.

The western wing remained with the IWW after the war; Covington Hall, alone of the prewar Wobbly leaders, was still active in the union as late as 1937.[16] It was the eastern industrial unionists who exiled themselves, were dispersed, jailed, disillusioned, or joined the Communists. With them went the unionist aspects of the IWW which were the characteristics most significant to the union's prewar successes. In a pamphlet published sometime during the twenties, the IWW mocked the eight-hour movement as a delusion. However excusable the movement might have been during "the childhood of the labor movement," the worker of the 1920s who advocated such a tactic was "insensible to the machine age in which he is living or he is a dishonest person." [17] This was a long way from the Wobbly stance in 1913 when only World War I interrupted the Wobblies' own projected eight-hour campaign.

The western capture of the IWW was not really completed until a few years after the war when the IWW's first infatuation with communism and the Russian Bolsheviks had dissolved amidst disillusion and bitterness. Many Wobblies were drawn to the Communist party after the Bolsheviks had assured their own survival; these converts were chiefly from the eastern wing. The reason for the development is obvious enough—the Communists had accomplished something. Jim Cannon wrote in a somewhat different context that it was a matter of success in Russia drawing adherents like flies.[18] In addition to Cannon, the Communist party inherited from the Wobblies Harrison George, George Mink, Elizabeth Gurley Flynn, John Reed, Harold Harvey, George Hardy, Charles Ashleigh, Ray Brown, Earl Browder, indirectly William Z. Foster, and, of course, Bill Haywood. According to Elizabeth Flynn, Cannon almost converted St. John to the new faith.[19]

Big Bill Haywood had told Ralph Chaplin, "the Russian Revolution is the greatest event in our lives. It represents all that we have been dreaming of and fighting for all our lives. It is the dawn of freedom and industrial democracy. If we can't trust Lenin, we can't trust anybody." Chaplin, who by his own account was skeptical of Bolshevism from the beginning, replied, "Does that mean you have made your choice?" Haywood said, "It means that there is only one choice to make. The world revolution is bigger than the IWW." [20] Later Haywood told Max Eastman the same thing: "The IWW reached out and grabbed an armful. It tried to grab the whole world, and a part of the world has jumped ahead of it." [21]

Many Wobblies, especially the westerners, did not share Haywood's enthusiasm, particularly after he was discredited by his defection to Moscow.[22] For a brief time, the *One Big Union Monthly* referred to "industrial Communism" instead of "industrial democracy" but the westerners such as Covington Hall protested loudly.[23] When the International ordered the IWW to change certain of its tactics in conformity with the strategy of the world revolution, the Wobblies balked, broke with the Communists, and to this day the two feeble organizations have been sharply critical of each other.

While the IWW's transformation and decline were hastened by wartime events, the process began even before the war. At the eighth convention in 1914 the decentralizers, or western wing, made an unsuccessful but strong bid for control of the organization. Their antagonists in the dispute were the leaders of the central office. The westerners' case for decentralizing the union along syndicalist lines was that each industrial area of the country had problems peculiar to itself and, thus, could best be settled locally.[24] This was a syndicalist position; ironically, at the same time that Haywood and the eastern Wobblies were being repudiated by the SPA as syndicalistic, they were battling syndicalists within the IWW.

The immediate occasion of the dispute was St. John's attacks on *The Lumberjack,* a quasi-syndicalist IWW paper which published several articles inciting sabotage. St. John called it "a Salvation Army sheet" and "not an IWW paper." Hall and St. John exchanged several notes, with the latter finally telling Hall that he "had no right to publish anything that was not sent by the National Office." [25]

St. John feared that the westerners might do great damage to the unionist aspects of the IWW. Hall claimed that the controversy was clearly sectional (another reason for decentralization) with "the West and the South backing me, and the East opposing. The Mississippi was the dividing line, due (I think) to the fact that the spirit of the frontiersman was still in the hearts of those west of the river; that there, liberty and not security, was the aim." [26] In 1914, the unionist eastern wing held its own, but the dispute illustrated the fact that the shifting nature of the IWW organization was already in progress before the war.

The dispersal of leadership, too, had begun before the war. Elizabeth Flynn and Carlo Tresca both broke with Haywood and the Wobblies during the Mesabi Range strike of 1915. While both later rushed back to do defense work for the imprisoned Wobblies in wartime, they had in reality left the organization before. St. John and Ettor had both begun to drop out of IWW activities as early as 1914. Pat Quinlan, a strike leader at Paterson, left jail in 1916 convinced that "direct action is not the way to win strikes—the only way to get relief is through politics." [27] Not long afterwards, Quinlan abandoned the idea of industrial unionism itself. Other old pro-Wobblies like Andre Tridon, William E. Walling, Robert R. LaMonte, J. G. Phelps Stokes, John Reed, and Walter Lippmann were already drifting away. William Z. Foster was long gone.

Haywood too was partially transformed even before the Sedition Act trials and the October Revolution. By 1915, disgusted with his treatment at the hands of the SPA, he began cantankerously to correct those who called the Wobblies Socialists, a name he had previously insisted upon. Richard Brazier wrote that even before the great trial of 1918 "there was something wrong with Haywood. He did not have the old fire he used to have. He talked in low tones, and had to be asked to speak a little louder now and then. It is my belief that Big Bill was even then sickening with the disease that finally did carry him off." [28] The IWW-SPA alliance had been crucial to Haywood's concept of eventual success. When it broke up, he began to fall apart just like the IWW.

In 1925, the IWW finally got around to admitting its decline and listed five reasons for the development. The bewildered state of the organization by that time was well illustrated by the contradictions in its reasoning. Thus, its first reason was that the immigration laws had given industry the chance to absorb the floating migratory labor among whom the IWW had been so successful. Then, contradicting the first, it cited the fact that over a million Mexican braceros in the Southwest "completely changed the type of unskilled labor" there. Third, the IWW named the second-hand Ford which made the family, not the individual male, the unit of labor in the West. One family made approximately what one man had made a decade before. Fourth, the completion of the construction boom had thrown many men out of work, and, fifth, it named the split in the IWW due to the Communists' siphoning off members.[29]

Four of the Wobblies' five reasons dealt specifically and exclusively with the western wing of the movement, the migrant workers. Not a word was said about the eastern wing which had actually been the most successful part of the prewar IWW. This was the best of indications that the westerners were in control. Moreover, there was little logic in the citation of greater exploitation (the Mexicans, family unit of labor) and unemployment in construction as factors making for Wobbly failure. The prewar IWW thrived in such situations; it hardly complained about them. The postwar IWW had simply given up.[30]

NOTES

1. Dan Wakefield, "The Haunted Hall: The IWW at Fifty," *Dissent* (1955).

2. "The General Strike," IWW pamphlet (Chicago, n.d.), IWW Collection, State Historical Society of Wisconsin.

3. William D. Haywood, *Bill Haywood's Book: The Autobiography of William D. Haywood* (New York: International Publishers, 1929), p. 299.

4. There are several excellent monographs on the topic of the wartime persecutions. Paul F. Brissenden, *The IWW: A Study of American Syndicalism* (New York: Russell & Russell, 1919); John S. Gambs, *The Decline of the I.W.W.* (New York: 1932; William Preston, Jr., *Aliens and Dissenters* (Cambridge: Harvard University Press, 1963); see also, Robert K. Murray, *Red Scare: A Study of National Hysteria* (Minneapolis: University of Minnesota Press 1964); Michael R. Johnson "The IWW and Wilsonian Democracy," *Science and Society* (Summer, 1964).

5. George Creel, "The American Newspaper," *Everybody's Magazine* 40 (1919): 43.

6. *Bill Haywood's Book,* p. 324.

7. Walter Lippmann, "The IWW: Insurrection or Revolution?," *New Review* 1 (August, 1913): 701.

8. "Evidence and Cross-Examination of William D. Haywood," (Chicago: IWW General Defense Committee, n.d.), p. 97.

9. Vincent St. John, *The IWW: Its History, Methods, and Structure* (New Castle, Pa. & Chicago: several editions), pp. 17–18. The idea of this comparison was conceived by Donald M. Barnes, "The Ideology of the Industrial Workers of the World: 1905–1921" (Ph.D. diss., Washington State University, 1962), p. 82. For a more extensive account of the IWW's wartime accommodation, see Joseph R. Conlin, *Big Bill Haywood and the Radical Union Movement* (Syracuse: Syracuse University Press, 1969).

10. Richard Brazier, to T. J. Bogard, n.d., Bogard Collection, Washington State Historical Society, quoted in Barnes, "Ideology of the IWW," p. 82.

11. Gambs, *Decline of the IWW*, pp. 91–92.

12. Quoted in Gambs, *Decline of the IWW*, p. 157.

13. Justus Ebert, *L'IWW Nella Teoria E Nella Pràtica* [The IWW in theory and practice] 5th rev. ed. (n.p., 1937), p. 107.

14. "One Big Union of All the Workers," IWW pamphlet (Chicago, n.d.), pp. 4–8; see also "New Turn of the IWW," *Socialist Review*, May, 1921; Marion D. Savage, *Industrial Unionism in America* (New York: Ronald Press Co., 1922), pp. 158–159.

15. Max Eastman, "Bill Haywood, Communist: An Interview," *The Liberator*, vol. 4 (April, 1921).

16. *One Big Union Monthly*, August, 1937.

17. "Industrial Unionism versus Anarchy and Reform," IWW pamphlet (Chicago, n.d.), IWW Collection, State Historical Society of Wisconsin.

18. James P. Cannon, *The IWW: The Great Infatuation* (New York: Pioneer Press, 1955), pp. 39–40.

19. Gambs, *Decline of the IWW*, p. 91; Cannon, "The IWW," pp. 39–40; Elizabeth Gurley Flynn, *I Speak My Own Piece: Autobiography of the Rebel Girl* (New York: International Publishing Co., 1955).

20. Ralph Chaplin, *Wobbly: The Rough and Tumble Story of an American Radical* (Chicago: University of Chicago Press, 1948), p. 298.

21. Eastman, "Bill Haywood," p. 14.

22. For one rank and file Wobbly's disappointment, see the Nicholas Steelinck Papers, Labor History Archives, Wayne State University.

23. *One Big Union Monthly* 1 (November, 1919): 29.

24. Covington Hall, "Labor Struggles in the Deep South," typescript, Labor History Archives, Wayne State University, p. 232.

25. Hall, "Labor Struggles," pp. 226–227.

26. Hall, "Labor Struggles," p. 227.

27. *Paterson Guardian*, November 24, 1916.

28. Richard Brazier, "The Great IWW Trial of 1918 in Retrospect," typescript, Labor History Archives, Wayne State University.

29. *Industrial Worker*, August 22, 1925.

30. William Z. Foster later listed several reasons, "internal weaknesses," which accounted for the failure of the IWW in his *History of the Communist Party of the United States* (New York: International Publishers, 1952), p. 112. They are not very informative; Foster appears more interested in providing a rationale for the Communist party than in seriously examining the Wobblies. For example, he notes the IWW's failure "to cultivate the political struggle of the working class," a misinterpretation which can only be construed to be Foster's way of defending the CPUSA's reliance on political action at the time when he wrote. In fact, the IWW was in informal alliance with the SPA while Foster's own Syndicalist League of North America was staunchly antipolitical. He also cites the IWW's reckless use of the general strike although the IWW called, in fact, only one, that in defense of Ettor and Giovannitti, a strictly one-day affair. He cites the Wobblies' incorrect handling of the religious question, for example, the "No God—No Master" poster at Lawrence. But this particular incident was not the work of the IWW but of a group of Boston anarchists. He mentions the "anarchistic decentralization" of the union but this was a characteristic of the IWW during the twenties after the movement had already declined. The prewar IWW was firmly committed to decentralized structure as the 1914 squabble illustrates. He cites correctly the IWW's "identification" with sabotage but this, as had been demonstrated, was not an "internal weakness" but something quite unfairly impressed upon the IWW from outside. As the leader of the Communist party, Foster should have better appreciated how the process of name-calling worked.

Note on Sources

To list every source consulted in the course of this study would duplicate and add negligibly to the footnotes. A brief description of the major research sources and books on the IWW and related subjects seems to be a better use of these pages. For a comprehensive bibliography of primary material, the reader is referred to Paul F. Brissenden, *The IWW: A Study of American Syndicalism* (New York: Russell & Russell, 1919), pp. 387–428.

The federal judge who during the 1920s ordered the confiscated files of the IWW destroyed did a great disservice to historians. By all descriptions, the files comprised a vast collection that would have been of invaluable use in answering many of the sticky questions the IWW poses to historians. As it is, the files are available only through the highly selective use to which federal prosecutors put them during the World War I Sedition trials. Nevertheless, various archivists have in recent years collected tangential or incomplete manuscripts that provide the historian with sources unavailable to early students of the movement. The Socialist Party of America Collection at Duke University is sketchy before 1911, when Carl D. Thompson organized the party's Information Department, but contains much of value relevant to the nature of the IWW's relationship with the SPA, the changing character of the party, the election of 1912, Haywood's recall in 1913, and the party's decline.

Some of the IWW's official files remain at the union's headquarters at 2422 N. Halsted Street in Chicago, but most have been transferred to the Labor History Archives at Wayne State University, which also holds several personal collections with material relating to the IWW. The State Historical Society of Wisconsin has a good collection of IWW pamphlets, as well as the papers of several Socialists who had some contact with the Wobblies, such as Daniel De Leon, Elizabeth Gurley Flynn, William English Walling, Adolph Germer, Morris Hillquit, and Algie and May Wood Simons.

Group 174 of the General Records of the Department of Labor at the National Archives consists of letters, memoranda, and reports of federal agents, some of which pertain to the IWW. Somewhat more valuable are the holdings of the Tamiment Institute in New York City, including some of the rarer IWW newspapers and some personal memorabilia. The Washington State Historical Society and the University of Washington have broad holdings relating to the Wobblies in the Northwest.

But by far the most important single repository for historians of the IWW is the Labadie Collection of the University of Michigan Library. The personal collection of Jo Labadie, a Michigan anarchist, maintained and expanded for many years by Miss Agnes Inglis, the collection is richest in regard to anarchism but comprehensive on the subjects of American socialism and the IWW as well.

The bulk of the Labadie and several other collections consists of Wobbly periodicals. The Wobblies were likely the most voracious readers that the American labor movement has ever known. The sociologist Carlton Parker observed that

considering their opportunity, the IWW read and discuss abstractions to a surprising extent. In their libraries the few novels are white-paged while a translation of Karl Marx or Kautsky, or the dull and theoretical pamphlets of their own leaders, are dog-eared.

Few American analysts have realized what firmly-held traditions have been established throughout all the working classes by the muckraking literature of the last twenty years.

Nels Anderson notes the same thing in his *The Hobo,* and an observer of a Wobbly trial in California reported that of eighty Wobblies who came to town to hear the trial, "not one of them went into a saloon," during the entire three weeks, "and the library at Marysville was hard beset to meet their demands for books." The IWW administration provided a number of periodicals and innumerable pamphlets to fulfill this demand. (One of the first actions of the IWW "local" in the Cook County jail during the Sedition trial was to produce a handwritten organ, "The Can Opener.") These periodicals are, of course, the necessary sources for understanding internal union developments, tactics, ideology, and Wobbly attitudes as well as providing an antidote for often biased newspaper accounts. To list them individually seems redundant. The reader is referred to Walter Goldwater's invaluable catalogue, *Radical Periodicals in America, 1890–1950* (New York: University Place, 1964).

Unpublished studies of the IWW, on the other hand, merit listing:

BARNES, DONALD M. *The Ideology of the Industrial Workers of the World 1905–1921.* Ph.D. dissertation, University of Washington, 1962.

BARNETT, EUGENE. *Centralia.* Personal narrative. Labadie Collection, University of Michigan Library.

BEFFEL, JOHN N. *Biographical Sketch of Joseph J. Ettor.* Personal reminiscence, February 25, 1948. Labor History Archives, Wayne State University Library.

BRAZIER, RICHARD. *The Great IWW Trial of 1918 in Retrospect.* Personal narrative. Labor History Archives, Wayne State University Library.

CONLIN, JOSEPH R. *The Wobblies: A Study of the IWW before World War I.* Ph.D. dissertation, University of Wisconsin, 1966.

CROW, JOHN E. *Ideology and Organization: A Case Study of the Industrial Workers of the World.* Master's thesis, University of Chicago, 1958.

FLYNN, ELIZABETH GURLEY. *Personal Recollections of the Industrial Workers of the World.* Tape recording of speech delivered at Northern Illinois University, November 8, 1962. Labor History Archives, Wayne State University Library.

FLYNN, ELIZABETH GURLEY. *The Truth About the Paterson Strike.* Typescript of speech delivered at the New York Civic Club Forum, January 31, 1914. Labadie Collection, University of Michigan Library.

HACKER, ABBE. *The Anarchist Influence on the IWW.* Typescript. Vertical File, Labadie Collection, University of Michigan Library.

HALL, COVINGTON. *Labor Struggles in the Deep South.* Personal narrative. Photostatic copy of typescript. Labor History Archives, Wayne State University Library.

HULL, ROBERT EDWARD. *IWW Activity in Everett, Washington from May, 1916 to June, 1917.* Master's thesis, Washington State College, 1938.

INGLIS, AGNES. *Reminiscences.* Manuscript, July 19, 1926. Vertical File, Labadie Collection, University of Michigan Library.

JENSEN, VERNON H. *Labor Relations in the Douglas Fir Industry.* Master's thesis, University of California, 1939.

PERRIN, ROBERT A. *Two Decades of Turbulence: A Study of the Great Lumber Strikes in Northern Idaho.* Master's thesis, University of Idaho, 1961.

PRESTON, WILLIAM. *The Ideology and Techniques of Repression: Government and the Radicals, 1903–1933.* Microfilm. University of Michigan.

SCHMIDT, DOROTHY NELL. *Sedition and Criminal Syndicalism in the State of Washington, 1917–1919.* Master's thesis, Washington State College, 1940.

STAVIS, BARRIE. *Joe Hill.* Typescript of a play, May 18, 1951. Labadie Collection, University of Michigan Library.

TYLER, ROBERT L. *Rebels of the Woods: A Study of the IWW in the Pacific Northwest.* Ph.D. dissertation, University of Oregon, 1953.

VOGEL, VIRGIL J. *The Historians and the Industrial Workers of the World.* Typescript, June 8, 1955, University of Chicago.

WEINTRAUB, HYMAN. *The IWW in California: 1905–1931*. Master's thesis, University of California, 1947.
WHITE, LAURA. *Rise of the Industrial Workers of the World*. Master's thesis, University of Nebraska, 1912.

Secondary literature on the IWW has happily been augmented of late. Brissenden's *IWW* remains standard but, as an informational source, it has been largely displaced by Philip S. Foner, *History of the Labor Movement in the United States* (New York: International Publishing Co., 1965), vol. 4, *The Industrial Workers of the World: 1905–1917*. Perhaps preferable as an introduction to the stuff of IWW history, however, is Patrick Renshaw, *The Wobblies: The Story of Syndicalism in the United States* (New York: Doubleday & Company, 1967) which, if it perpetuates some myths about its subject, is a highly readable volume. Robert S. Tyler, *Rebels of the Woods: The IWW in the Pacific Northwest* (Eugene, Ore.: University of Oregon Books, 1968) is also a well-written account of the IWW in that region where they were once significant. Fred Thompson, *The IWW: Its First Fifty Years* (Chicago: IWW Publishing Bureau, 1955) is an anniversary volume published by the IWW and includes a great deal of valuable information. Joyce Kornbluh, *Rebel Voices* (Ann Arbor: University of Michigan Press, 1964) is a large and well-edited volume of Wobbly writings and graphics.

Biographies and autobiographies of persons who figure in these pages are abundant. Most notable is William D. Haywood's autobiography, *Bill Haywood's Book* (New York: International Publishers, 1929) and the writer has written an analytical study of the Wobbly leader, *Big Bill Haywood and the Radical Union Movement* (Syracuse: 1969). Others, by no means all, include Fred E. Beal, *Proletarian Journey* (New York: Hillman-Curl, 1937); Ralph Chaplin, *Wobbly: The Rough and Tumble Story of an American Radical* (Chicago: University of Chicago Press, 1948); Elizabeth G. Flynn, *I Speak My Own Piece* (New York: International Publishing Co., 1955); William Z. Foster, *From Bryan to Stalin* (London: Lawrence & Wishart, 1937); Ray Ginger, *The Bending Cross: A Biography of Eugene V. Debs* (New Brunswick: The Macmillan Co., Collier Books, 1949); Emma Goldman, *Living My Life* (New York:

A. A. Knopf, 1931); Samuel Gompers, *Seventy Years of Life and Labor* (New York: Kelley, 1925); George Hardy, *Those Stormy Years* (London: Lawrence & Wishart, 1956); Dona Torr, *Tom Mann and His Times* (London: Lawrence & Wishart, 1936).

On American socialism, the best survey volume is David A. Shannon, *The American Socialist Party: A History* (New York: The Macmillan Co., 1955). Ira Kipnis, *The American Socialist Movement: 1897–1912* (New York: Columbia University Press, 1952) was especially valuable. And a persuasive modification of previous analyses is James Weinstein, *The Decline of Socialism in America* (New York: Monthly Review Press, 1967).

There are, finally, two dozen scholarly articles on the IWW of particular merit or peculiar interest:

BLAISDELL, LOWELL L. "Was It Revolution or Filibustering? The Magon Revolt in Baja California." *Pacific Historical Review,* vol. 23 (May, 1954).

BOTTING, DAVID C. "Bloody Sunday." *Pacific Northwest Quarterly,* vol. 49 (October, 1958).

DOHERTY, ROBERT E. "Thomas J. Hagerty, the Church, and Socialism." *Labor History,* vol. 3 (Winter, 1962).

ELLIOTT, RUSSELL R. "Labor Troubles in the Mining Camp at Goldfield, Nevada, 1906–1908." *Pacific Historical Review,* vol. 19 (November, 1950).

GERHARD, PETER. "The Socialist Invasion of Baja California, 1911." *Pacific Historical Review,* vol. 15 (September, 1946).

HAWLEY, JAMES H. "Steve Adams' Confession and the State's Case Against Bill Haywood." *Idaho Yesterdays,* vol. 7 (Winter, 1963–64).

HOXIE, ROBERT F. "The Socialist Party in the November Elections." *Journal of Political Economy,* vol. 20 (March, 1912).

HOXIE, ROBERT F. "The Truth About the IWW." *Journal of Political Economy,* vol. 20 (March, 1912).

JOHNSON, MICHAEL R. "The IWW and Wilsonian Democracy." *Science and Society,* vol. 28 (Summer, 1964).

KENDALL, JOHN S. "New Orleans' 'Peculiar Institution.'" *Louisiana Historical Quarterly,* vol. 23 (July, 1940).

LEVINE, LOUIS. "Development of Syndicalism in America." *Political Science Quarterly*, vol. 28 (September, 1913).

MC KEE, DON K. "Daniel De Leon: A Reappraisal." *Labor History*, vol. 1 (1960).

MC WHINEY, GRADY. "Louisiana Socialists in the Early Twentieth Century: A Study of Rustic Radicalism." *Journal of Southern History*, vol. 20 (August, 1954).

NEWMAN, PHILIP. "The First IWW Invasion of New Jersey." *Proceedings of the New Jersey Historical Society*, vol. 58 (October, 1940).

SCHEINBERG, STEPHEN. "The Haywood Trial: Theodore Roosevelt's Undesirable Citizens." *Idaho Yesterdays*, vol. 4 (Fall, 1960).

STAVIS, BARRIE. "Joe Hill: Poet/Organizer." *Folk Music* (June–August, 1964).

TAFT, PHILIP. "The IWW in the Grain Belt." *Labor History*, vol. 1 (Winter, 1960).

TYLER, ROBERT L. "The Everett Free Speech Fight." *Pacific Historical Review*, vol. 23 (February, 1954).

TYLER, ROBERT L. "The IWW in the Pacific Northwest: Rebels in the Woods." *Oregon Historical Quarterly*, vol. 55 (March, 1954).

TYLER, ROBERT L. "The IWW and the West." *American Quarterly*, vol. 11 (Summer, 1960).

TYLER, ROBERT L. "The Rise and Fall of American Radicalism." *The Historian*, vol. 19 (November, 1956).

WAKEFIELD, DAN. "The Haunted Hall: The IWW at Fifty." *Dissent* (1955).

WHITTEN, WOODROW S. "The Wheatland Episode." *Pacific Historical Review*, vol. 17 (February, 1948).

Index

161

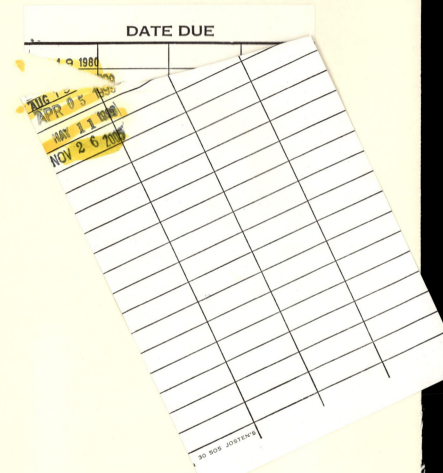